LIFELINE ACROSS THE SEA

LIFELINE ACROSS THE SEA

MERCY SHIPS OF THE SECOND WORLD WAR
AND THEIR REPATRIATION MISSIONS

DAVID L. WILLIAMS

Cover illustrations
Front: Vulcania off Gibraltar. (Mario Cicogna); *back:* Nurses greet mercy ship *Djenné* from the quayside at Marseille. (Klaus Günther von Martinez collection)

First published 2015

The History Press
The Mill, Brimscombe Port
Stroud, Gloucestershire, GL5 2QG
www.thehistorypress.co.uk

British Library Cataloguing in Publication Data.
A catalogue record for this book is available from the British Library.

ISBN 978 0 7509 6135 6

Typesetting and origination by The History Press
Printed in Malta by Melita Press.

CONTENTS

ACKNOWLEDGEMENTS

It would not have been possible to complete a project such as this, which draws on archive material distributed all around the world, without assistance from many correspondents, colleagues and enthusiasts, and I would like here to acknowledge those persons and organisations for their valued contributions. It is thanks to their generosity with photographs that would otherwise have been difficult to locate, and the benefit of their specialised and detailed knowledge of the careers of some of the less well-known ships, that this extensive account of the wartime mercy ships has been made possible.

Accordingly, I would like to put on record my warmest appreciation of the help I received from: Jean-Yves Brouard, Michael Cassar, Nereo Castelli, Luis Miguel Correia, Mario Cicogna, Lars Hemingstam, Richard de Kerbrech, Anibal José Maffeo, Carlos Mey, Peter Newall, the late Luca Ruffato, and Paolo Valenti.

Besides those individuals, a number of institutions have graciously supported my efforts, among them the following, with recognition of their members of staff who assisted me: British Pathé (Ruth Cahir), British Red Cross HQ, London (Jane High), Bündesarchiv (Martina Caspers), Deutsches Schiffahrtsmuseum (Klaus Fuest), East Asiatic Co. (Erik Ljunggren), Guildhall Library, Histarmar, Museu Maritim di Barcelona (Javier Aznar), National Archives, News UK Group Publishing Services (Nick Mays), NYK Maritime Museum (Hakuei Wakiya), International Committee of the Red Cross, Geneva (Daniel Palmieri and his staff), Sjöfartsmuseet Akvariet (Cilla Ingvarsson), Swedish Red Cross (Sonja Sjöstrand), United States National Archives & Records Administration (Kim McKeithan), World Ship Society (Jim McFaul and Tony Smith) and WZ-Bilddienst Bildarchiv (Sibylle Jaspers).

Last but not least, I would like to express my thanks to Amy Rigg of The History Press for her invaluable support and guidance.

INTRODUCTION

Behind the scenes during the Second World War, a series of agreements were concluded through negotiations between the combatants whereby prisoners, usually wounded or gravely ill, 'protected personnel' – doctors, nurses, stretcher bearers, ambulance crews and other medical personnel, as well as chaplains – and diplomats, civilians and alien internees could be safely exchanged. It is a dimension of the war at sea about which, with few exceptions, little is widely known. Working through neutral intermediaries and conducted under the auspices of the International Red Cross, deals were reached individually between the United Kingdom and each of the Axis belligerents, Germany, Italy and Japan. Likewise, such exchanges were also arranged with the Axis by the United States and other Allied nations.

Some thirty or so repatriation missions, derived primarily from the rules of the Geneva Convention, took place during the war, while more than fifty ships, both Allied and Axis, defined as specific types of 'Safe-passage' vessels by the Hague Convention and other maritime law, were engaged in the highly dangerous work of sailing undefended and invariably alone through hostile waters to deliver their precious human cargoes. Mainly former passenger liners, they were supported by short-sea vessels and train ferries as well as some cargo ships, many of them adorned in unique livery. At night, they were required to be brightly illuminated, making them strangely conspicuous when most ships were seeking concealment. The ships were constantly at risk of erroneous attack by submarine or aircraft, their safety and security depending totally on the transmission and receipt of unambiguous commands to the armed units in their paths stipulating that they should be allowed to proceed unharmed. The vagaries of war circumstances, the possibility of misidentification in inclement weather and the still relatively primitive nature of radio equipment at that time, prone to interference and restricted in its use to prevent detection, all combined together to magnify the hazards. The prospect of attack and severe loss of life were a constant cause of anxiety for those involved in these operations.

To set the scene, in order to appreciate the complexities and potential issues that surrounded these humanitarian efforts, some of the legal and organisational framework requires explanation – the nature and work of the facilitating institutions, the types of protected ship and the criteria and mechanisms whereby persons qualifying for exchange were selected.

Those endangered persons from whom potential repatriates could be drawn were both numerous and various in character. Warfare, no matter what its intensity or duration, can throw up thousands, even millions, of displaced persons of a variety of descriptions. In the Second World War, within all the belligerent countries, there were countless numbers of those who were either directly affected by the conflict or who became victims of security clampdowns on the outbreak of hostilities. Quite apart from refugees seeking shelter from the violence, there were many other civilian categories at threat, either trapped or incarcerated. Among them were enemy aliens, ex-patriot and domiciled foreigners who previously had been accepted by a domestic population but who, at the onset of hostilities, were rounded-up and interned. In Britain around 80,000 aliens were identified who potentially presented a security risk. The vast majority were interned in camps on the Isle of Man. Over 7,000 were subsequently deported to Australia and Canada, a risky business as substantiated by several high-profile losses to U-boat attack, among them the *Arandora Star* with 805 casualties, the majority Italians, and the *Empress of Canada* from which another 392 were killed.

The *Arandora Star* was sunk west of the Bloody Foreland on 2 July 1940 while bound from Liverpool to Canada with Italian and German internees. Lacking safe-conduct protection, she was a legitimate target for U-47. *Maritime Photo Library*

In the case of the *Empress of Canada*, sunk on 14 March 1943, she was loaded with both refugees and Italian prisoners, many of whom perished. *Author's collection*

In Germany, millions of Jewish civilians were sent to concentration camps along with the political opponents of the Nazis and members of minority religious orders. When war broke out in the Far East, the American Government implemented a major programme of arrest and internment of 100,000 Japanese-Americans, often in poor conditions, and between 1941 and 1942 more than 130,000 civilians of British, American, Dutch and Commonwealth origin who were living and working in invaded territories were incarcerated by the Japanese. Last, but not least, arising from the normal process of exchange of embassy and consular staff, there were the diplomats located in foreign embassies and consulates, along with their families. Often the last to leave because their essential services were required to the end, they were frequently and unavoidably left stranded within enemy borders when diplomatic relations were severed or war was declared.

Where service personnel were concerned, by far the most numerous category were the countless prisoners of war (POW) taken during combat, mainly men – soldiers captured on the battlefield, crew members taken as survivors of sunken warships or air crews shot down over enemy territory – all imprisoned in camps. Significantly, many of these persons qualified for repatriation to their homelands, but the formal provisions for doing this really only existed in respect of seriously sick or invalided POW, under the auspices of the Geneva Convention of 1929. The rights of these persons to repatriation, if any, can be summarised as follows:

The only POW entitled to be repatriated were those selected by medical boards (see below) in accordance with the rules agreed bilaterally by the opposing nations. Governed by the directives of the Geneva Convention, it was not essential for there to be equivalence in the numbers exchanged.

Protected personnel were entitled by right to repatriation under the Geneva Convention but could be refused if the power holding them considered that, by releasing them, there would be insufficient medical personnel left to tend the remaining sick and injured prisoners.

Merchant seamen, taken off ships seized in foreign ports or arrested on the high seas, were an anomalous group given their strategic value, serving either on auxiliaries or crewing vital convoy supply ships. Germany treated them as civilians and sought to have parity of numbers in exchanges. Great Britain, in contrast, treated them as either POW or civilians depending on whether they were apprehended by military or civil authorities.

Civilians, including internees, who desired to be repatriated had no basic rights of return. The decision to make such exchanges depended on negotiation and agreement through diplomatic channels between the opposing nations, conducted via nominated intermediaries. The numbers of persons for exchange were intended to be equal, i.e. on a head-for-head basis, although that was not always the case. As a point of interest, those non-governmental civilians who were repatriated were expected to pay for their passage. The United States, as an example, arranged a flat-rate fare, something which proved rather contentious because the standard of accommodation on the ships, as in peacetime, varied considerably by class.

For civilians, it was a question of persuading the combatants to apply the principles of military repatriation to non-military candidates, and in that respect the influence and involvement of the International Committee of the Red Cross (ICRC) was both fundamental and critical in order to make any sort of progress. From the outset, the ICRC in Geneva made it known that it intended to proactively pursue the implementation of repatriation programmes both for military prisoners and civilians. 'The Work of the International Committee of the Red Cross during the Second World War' states:

> From the outbreak of hostilities, the repatriation of seriously wounded or sick POW formed part of the main activities which the ICRC set itself to carry out in behalf of war victims. This intention was notified to the belligerent states on September 4, 1939, in the first circular letter addressed to them.

Repeatedly thereafter, the ICRC alerted combatants to their responsibilities in respect of POW, called for reciprocal treatment of civilian internees and worked to have humanitarian provision extended to embrace older and long-term prisoners who otherwise were in good health. Much praise and credit must go to that organisation for the successful achievement of most of those aims.

Much the same applies to the various national Red Cross organisations as well as to the governments of those neutral countries that made their port facilities available as safe havens where exchanges of personnel could be conducted without fear of military intervention. Principal among them were Sweden, Portugal, Spain and Turkey.

Few, if any, of the exchange and repatriation missions that took place were without complications of one sort or another, if only beset by protracted and sensitive negotiations. Even where repatriations of service personnel were concerned, there was often a measure of distrust between the parties involved that could potentially hamper the process of exchange, difficulties that were eased by the delicate intervention of intermediaries who encouraged and assisted negotiations and who strove to ensure the continuation of sustainable exchange mechanisms. In principle those that involved military personnel stood a better chance of succeeding, being aided by the preordained rules and conditions of the Geneva Convention of 1929, which were intended to smooth the process. The Convention had been signed by four of the main combatants, namely Great Britain, the USA, Germany and Italy. While Japan had signed the agreement but declined to ratify it, the country had indicated a preparedness to observe the spirit of its intentions and to implement it in practice. In many respects, subsequent events would rightly challenge the integrity of those declarations, but it has to be said that Japan did participate actively, albeit minimally, in the ICRC-led programme of repatriation.

Articles 68 to 74 of the Geneva Convention are the ones that specifically relate to wartime repatriation, outlining the internationally agreed rights and responsibilities of the belligerent signatories (referred to as the Detaining Powers) in respect of the return to their home country or a neutral state of those prisoners-of-war who qualified for repatriation. Article 68 states:

> Belligerents shall be required to send back to their own country, without regard to rank or numbers, after rendering them in a fit condition for transport, prisoners-of-war who are seriously ill or seriously wounded. Agreements between the belligerents should determine as soon as possible, the forms of disablement or sickness requiring direct repatriation and cases which may necessitate accommodation in a neutral country.

The post-war report of the ICRC ('Rapport du Comité International de la Croix-Rouge sur son activité pendant la seconde guerre mondiale, 1 septembre 1939 – 30 juin 1947'), hereafter referred to as ICRC-1948, is valuable in explaining how the repatriation of civilians was also pursued, drawing on the principles and practices of the relevant Geneva Convention articles wherever appropriate. ICRC-1948 highlights these efforts under the section 'Repatriation During Hostilities':

> During hostilities, the repatriation of civilians, whether interned or not, was generally through diplomatic channels, that is to say, through the Protecting Powers [see below]. The ICRC had sometimes, however, to take action in this field, either because diplomatic negotiations seemed to lead to no result, or because its intervention had been asked for, or because it availed itself of the initiative accorded by custom in humanitarian questions, and thought fit to act in cases that seemed especially to merit its attention.

Repeated circulars were transmitted to the warring nations urging the general repatriation of civilians, proposing that the benefits of Articles 68 to 74 of the Geneva Convention, often referred to as the 'Prisoner-of-War Code', should also be applied to non-combatants and internees, in particular the provisions of Article 72, which dealt with cases of captivity of long duration.

To facilitate the implementation of such operations and, where exchanges of non-military nationals did occur, the ICRC offered and provided escorts for ships and trains carrying civilian internee repatriates. It should be borne in mind that the Geneva Convention bestowed a special role upon the ICRC whereby it became the internationally recognised body responsible for matters relating to the handling of service prisoners in wartime, including being granted access to the sick and wounded as well as stewardship in cases of exchange and transfer. It was reasonable for the organisation to endeavour to extend this role to embrace civilians as well as military personnel, and it is as well that it did.

The provisions of the Geneva Convention like other similar agreements constitute international law insofar as the treatment of prisoners in wartime is concerned. Therefore, it is useful to provide definitions of some of the terms used in the Convention:

Protecting Powers

Formalised in the Convention, these are the nation states that represent the interests of the Detaining Powers (the belligerents – otherwise referred to as the Protected States or Host States) where normal diplomatic relations have been severed. Each Protecting Power was appointed by a Detaining Power but had to be acceptable to the opposing Detaining Power. In all cases they were required to be neutral countries, neither engaged in any way in the conflict nor party to any treaties with a Detaining Power that could compromise their impartiality. As an example, the USA was initially appointed, in agreement with Germany, as the Protecting Power for Great Britain. However, when America entered the war in December 1941, following the Japanese attack on Pearl Harbor, it relinquished this role and from that time Switzerland assumed the position of Protecting Power for Great Britain. In particular Protecting Powers acted as go-betweens where the welfare of prisoners was concerned.

Mixed Medical Commissions (MMC)

These were the bodies responsible for determining on medical grounds those who would be approved or declined for repatriation. Their composition and function are detailed in Articles 69 and 70 respectively. They were to comprise three members, two from a neutral country and one appointed by the Detaining Power. The precise procedures for the implementation and conduct of MMC were not explicitly defined in the Convention, but it was anticipated that, aided by the Protecting Powers and the ICRC, satisfactory arrangements would be agreed between the opposing Detaining Powers. The preference was for all MMC delegates to be practising doctors, but this could not be achieved in all instances. Likewise, it was not always possible to appoint two delegates of neutral citizenship, especially where a belligerent was remote (e.g. Australia). Under the auspices of the ICRC, acceptable Swiss doctors were frequently co-opted onto MMC in place of neutral delegates.

Draft Model Agreement (full and correct title: Model Agreement Concerning Direct Repatriation of Prisoners-of-War for Reasons of Health)

Outlined in an annex to Article 68 of the Geneva Convention, this provided the governing principles as to the medical conditions, their gravity and duration that would qualify those so affected for repatriation. It was intended to provide the framework from which an agreement could be reached between Detaining Powers and its use was recommended by the ICRC.

Protected Ship Types

Central to the contents of this volume, these are the categories of ship employed for the physical conveyance of repatriates to and from the ports of exchange under protected, safe-conduct or safe-passage status. Vessels of each type were nominated, registered and endorsed by the relevant Detaining Powers although the rules regarding their function and mode of operation were not defined in the Geneva Convention. There were two categories involved in the performance of repatriation and exchange missions in the Second World War:

The first category was hospital ships, as defined under Article 4 of the Hague Convention of 1907. All hospital ships had to be registered with the ICRC at Geneva, which also notified all concerned parties of the identity of these ships, providing details of their names, their general appearance and distinctive characteristics. They were to be unarmed and were not to be used for any military purpose, nor were they permitted to interfere in any way with enemy combatant vessels. While belligerents had the right to investigate suspected violations of the restrictions under which hospital ships were operated, to deliberately attack or sink any such ship that complied with the agreed regulations was deemed to be a war crime. Where the wartime repatriation operations were concerned some already-designated hospital ships were utilised, either wholly or part-time, for certain exchanges, temporarily withdrawn from their defined role of tending to and transporting the sick and wounded military personnel of their flag nationality. While they became subject to modified rules of conduct to those normally applicable to hospital ships, for all practical purposes their status and appearance remained unchanged. Hospital ships were painted in standard colours, regardless of the national flag they were operating under. These colours are described in Chapter 2, The Mercy Missions.

The majority of the vessels that undertook 'mercy' repatriation missions during the Second World War fell in the category of cartel ships. Defined under international maritime law, this was a type of ship recognised as being engaged in the transportation of prisoners on specially arranged humanitarian voyages between named ports at which exchanges were to take place. Accordingly, they were afforded protection, that is they were temporarily exempted from capture or attack, with their inviolability extended to both outward and return voyages in each instance as well as to their time in port. They included neutral ships taken up under charter. The cartel from which the ships' designation was derived was a form of agreement entered into by parties engaged in armed conflict for the exchange of POW or humanitarian aid, effectively a mechanism in its broadest sense whereby actions and relations of a non-hostile nature could be arranged, regulated and conducted between otherwise belligerent powers.

A complication of the cartel ship category which can be somewhat confusing is that, whereas its existence was usually the result of a bilateral arrangement, it may have and often did require additional 'safe-passage' or 'safe-conduct' clearance from third-party belligerents or neutral countries through whose waters or a recognised war zone it had reason to pass in the execution of its mission. Typically, cartel ships did not adopt a standard mode of livery. The majority were painted in distinctive colour schemes that were largely unique in character, in many cases variations on a theme in that they frequently displayed the 'Cross' symbol though not always red in colour. These markings are also described later in the Missions chapter.

Certain of the ships that participated in the repatriation missions, and which are described in the following pages, may not have been in either of the categories defined above. In the absence of detailed records or contemporary photographs it is impossible to say for certain whether or not they were protected ships, but without acknowledged protection their occupants would have been placed at considerable risk for the duration of the voyages concerned. The ships that fall into this grey area generally participated in an ancillary capacity, either operating between ports on short-sea routes as part of the actual exchanges or, indirectly, by conveying interned aliens to deep-sea ports where they could be embarked upon designated repatriation ships.

Unlike those that applied normally to hospital ships, the rules of engagement for cartel ships and hospital ships while temporarily deployed on repatriation missions were agreed individually by the Detaining Powers party to each exchange agreement. Like hospital ships, cartel ships had to be illuminated at night to highlight their special protective markings and prevent misidentification. Generally, all repatriation ships were required to sail independently and alone on pre-determined courses, entering and leaving ports of call on stipulated dates. All such details were relayed to the combatant vessels operating in the sea areas to be crossed. They were also required not to zigzag but to navigate a steady course and maintain a steady speed, and they were required to transmit their midday position over a selected international frequency daily. The attention to detail that was given to every aspect of the repatriation voyages, as the contents of the files in the National Archives reveals, was astonishing. Everything from the precise routes to be navigated, by compass bearing and distance, the victualling and bunkering arrangements (a particularly acute concern was replenishment of water supplies while operating in the tropics), and the careful adjudication of every passenger – their number, gender and condition as well as, based on intelligence, any threat they may have posed.

Such precise control measures were typical but perfectly understandable. Deviations from agreed arrangements were not, for the most part, tolerated, simply because of the massive effort required to re-plan every minute detail, taking into consideration tide, weather and technical issues, besides the impact of continuing or imminent military action in areas to where the ships were travelling or destined. There was always the concern, too, that any deviation, deliberate or otherwise, could undermine trust and the willingness to continue with repatriation missions, as well as potentially place those en route in heightened danger. An incident that occurred during the September 1944 exchange at Gothenburg highlights this particularly well.

When two or three British soldiers who had escaped from Germany and managed to reach Sweden stowed away aboard the *Arundel Castle*, almost certainly with the connivance of the soldiers being repatriated, their misguided though well-intentioned action threatened serious consequences. Having made the mistake of leaving their hiding place and declaring themselves soon after the ship left port, though she was still in Swedish waters, they did not get the reception they had anticipated. They had unintentionally put the ship and all aboard her at serious risk because the agreed arrangement had been to exchange a precise number of service personnel, no more, no less. The unofficial presence of these extra men potentially rendered void the ship's protected status and had it become known to the German authorities, they could have seized the ship and everybody aboard her. There was no alternative but to hand the British soldiers over to the escorting Swedish destroyer for internment in Sweden.

Nonetheless, despite this unpopular but essential action there were still repercussions. As the transfer to the Swedish destroyer had been observed, the very moment the ship left Swedish waters it was boarded by a German naval party and a contingent of German troops. All the POW aboard the *Arundel Castle*, as well as her entire crew, were mustered on deck for a roll call and head count. Stretcher cases were allowed to remain below, but otherwise the accommodation areas were completely vacated while a thorough search took place. After a long delay, but to the relief of the ship's company, the count was pronounced correct and the ship was eventually allowed to proceed.

For both sides in the war, there were potential downsides to the participation in 'mercy voyages' despite the worthiness of these missions. For one thing, it meant a commitment of limited shipping resources that were preferably needed for other essential wartime employment while it could also reveal to an enemy a measure of a combatant's shipping strength. In the greater scheme of things, national efforts were primarily concentrated on securing victory and these humanitarian operations were probably considered little more than a sideshow to the main business of the day. The reluctance of service chiefs to release valuable tonnage, particularly at a time when major amphibious landings were planned, is understandable.

Of course, there were other matters of concern associated with running repatriation exchanges besides stowaways, among them smuggling, especially of small-scale high-value war materials, and espionage, the gathering of sensitive military information through observations at ports of call. The primary mechanism for managing these risks was the system of Contraband Control operated at strategic locations under the general implementation of blockade measures. Under these, all merchant vessels were liable to examination and, if found aboard them, the confiscation of ammunition, explosives, chemicals, fuel, communication equipment, machinery, tools, foodstuffs, animal feed, bullion, currency, gemstones and so on. This presented difficulties where some repatriation ships were concerned, potentially interfering with strict voyage plans or creating delays. To overcome such problems, Britain introduced the issue of warrants or NaviCerts (Navigational Certificates) for neutral flagships and certain Allied vessels, a system that originated in the First World War, whereby they could be examined and cleared for passage in their port of origin.

Despite the hazards and inconveniences, there were tangible benefits for those nations engaged in repatriation, not least of which, quite apart from the obvious one of getting citizens and sick servicemen home, was the positive contribution to morale on the home front, which could not be underestimated.

In that regard, it is of interest to note that the participant nations frequently insisted upon confidentiality as a condition of these operations, possibly because the release of prisoners, whatever their state of health, may have been interpreted as an act of weakness or a stance incompatible with the national mood. Author P. Scott Corbett called the repatriation missions the 'Quiet Passages'. However, despite this insistence on judicious discretion, in fact they were often widely reported in the press and routinely covered by newsreel cameramen.

In order to convey the full range and extent of the repatriation endeavours, this book has been written from the perspective of the repatriation ships and the missions undertaken by them during the Second World War, that is between September 1939 and September 1945. The aim here is to present as fully and accurately as possible a record of all the ships involved both directly and indirectly in wartime mercy missions. Also, to the extent that available records

The *President Coolidge* in Dollar Line colours. With her sister ship, she was sent on a special mission to Yangtze ports in August 1937 to assist in the repatriation of American citizens during the Sino-Japanese War, a precursor to the Second World War missions. *A. Palmer*

Docked at the Dollar Line pier at Los Angeles, sister ship *President Hoover*. During the 1937 repatriation mission, she was attacked by Chinese warplanes, which mistakenly identified her as a Japanese transport. *Bill Miller*

While the two Dollar Lines' ships retrieved US personnel, at the same time the P&O liner *Rajputana* performed a similar task, picking up British citizens from Nanking and Shanghai. *Author's collection*

permit, it is an account of their chronological movements on each of the voyages they undertook. However, it should be stressed that the book cannot be claimed to be comprehensive in that respect, partly because there may have been other missions that have not come to light but also because, despite extensive research, some dates remain elusive or unconfirmed and, specifically, some ships remain unidentified.

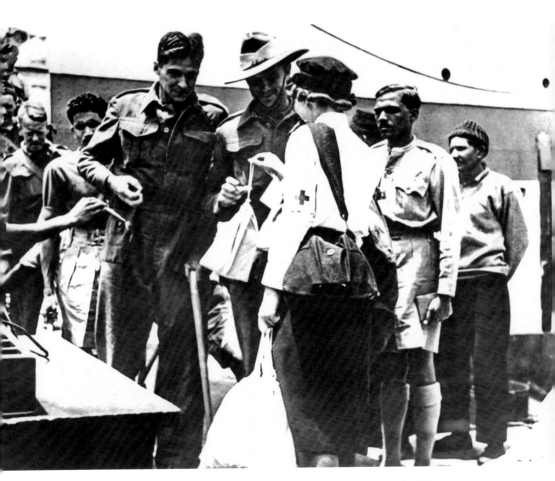

Repatriated prisoners of war disembark into the care of waiting nurses. The ship is unidentified. *British Red Cross*

1

THE MERCY SHIPS

A total of forty-nine ships have been identified as having participated, either directly or indirectly, in the thirty or so mercy missions of the Second World War, covering both military repatriations and the exchanges of diplomats, interned civilians and Protected Personnel.

The descriptions that follow provide the technical particulars and concise details of the peacetime commercial employment of these ships, as well as of other activities undertaken by them during the war prior to their engagement for repatriation duties. Another, separate group of seven Swedish vessels were among others deployed on special humanitarian missions in the Baltic just before and after the end of the war in Europe.

There are undoubtedly other ships that, despite significant research, have not been positively revealed and which, therefore, are not included herein. In fact, certain official documents make tantalising reference to other maritime transport engaged in elements of these missions, but the vessels' names have not been disclosed. Without examining in detail every movement of every ship, if such records still exist, it is impossible now to identify those vessels. Among those whose identities remain unknown are some of the ferries used for the carriage of repatriates to and from main ports of embarkation and disembarkation. Where appropriate, however, such references to unnamed ships have been incorporated in the narrative of the individual missions concerned in order to provide the most complete account possible.

Given the nature of the duties of some of these ships, it is evident that not all vessels described here necessarily functioned under the auspices of the International Red Cross, either at all, partially or even temporarily. This applies principally to the smaller vessels that conveyed repatriates to and from ports under the control of the same belligerent, where they were then transferred onto or off bigger ships. It also pertains to certain of the larger ships whose total deployment may not have been arranged under protective cover as cartel ships or whose entire voyages did not fall within the protective provisions agreed between two belligerents. Where longer-distance sea travel was concerned, some exchange prisoners first proceeded aboard ships under 'safe-passage', as far as the

Eighth Army prisoners captured during the desert campaign in North Africa and who had escaped from Italian camps and crossed into Switzerland were repatriated in October 1944 aboard the *Eastern Prince*, which retained her standard troopship colours and sailed in convoy. This view of the *Eastern Prince* dates from later. *Maritime Photo Library*

point where formal protection terminated only to continue or be transferred to other vessels to complete their journey home without any agreed immunity from attack. In that regard, a ship that should be mentioned here is the *Eastern Prince* (1929/10,926grt) built by Napier & Miller, Glasgow (yard no. 266), for Furness Prince Line's service from New York to La Plata ports. Although, in 1944, she carried home repatriated POW, specifically men of the Eighth Army who had been held in Italian prison camps, she was not a mercy ship as such, nor was she engaged directly in a recognised repatriation mission.

The Eighth Army personnel concerned had all escaped from their camps and crossed into Switzerland where they had been interned. Their presence was something of an embarrassment for the Swiss, whose unique humanitarian status risked being compromised. To return the escapees to Italy – presumably the action that should have been taken – would have conflicted with the country's declared values, the men having suffered miserably in the camps. However, to retain them within its borders could undermine relations with Germany, something that was important to avoid for the benefit of other exchange missions then under discussion.

To overcome the dilemma, the Swiss adopted a pragmatic approach, ensuring their services were indispensable to both sides. This permitted it to invoke certain repatriations in its own right. Described as Swiss Direct Governmental Repatriation Agreements, they enabled action to be taken to safely remove the presence of compromising aliens who were also a burden on the state's limited resources, having to be fed and accommodated at its expense. Several such repatriations took place, mainly overland, but the release and return of the Eighth Army escapees was partly by sea, probably from Marseilles, after they had been taken there by train. Contemporary Pathé news film, *Back to Blighty* (ID: 1366.32), shows the *Eastern Prince* arriving with the returning soldiers at a British north-west port, probably Glasgow, in October 1944, but the commentary does not state from where they set out. The ship itself, which was unmarked and painted in accordance with the standard troopship colours of the day – the Admiralty Standard Grey Concealment Scheme for Merchant Ships, comprising the grey shades MSS (Merchant Ships Side) and MSD (Merchant Ships Deck) with white funnel top and mast tops – had sailed from Algiers in a routine convoy, MKF 35, escorted by warships. Of course, in these circumstances, without any safe-passage clearance, she constituted a legitimate target for attack.

The *El Nil*, used in the Lourenço Marques exchange (see Mission 11), is also believed to have delivered home repatriated servicemen in this fashion at some time in 1943 before she became a hospital ship. Another Pathé film, *Wounded Returning Home* (ID: 1943.02), shows her arriving at Liverpool. Although she is not named, she can be identified from her features. Of significance, it can be clearly seen that she is not carrying protective markings but is painted navy grey, her lower hull somewhat darker than her upper works, suggesting one of the Admiralty Alternative colour schemes adopted for use by troopships.

Moored in the Grand harbour, Valletta, on 28 October 1949, the Ministry of Transport (MoT) troopship *El Nil. Michael Cassar*

The last chapter of the book briefly summarises for each of the ships described below their post-mission fates or subsequent careers through to the end of their working lives.

Repatriation Ships

AQUILEIA ex *Prins der Nederlanden (1935) Lloyd Triestino*

9,448grt; 498ft LOA; 57ft beam
Nederlandsche Schps. Maats., Amsterdam (yard no. 123)
Quadruple-expansion steam reciprocating, twin screw

January 1914: completed for Nederland Royal Mail Line's Amsterdam–Dutch East Indies service via Suez; sister ship, *Koningin Emma*. **1935**: sold to Lloyd Triestino for service from Trieste to Africa and the Far East. **May 1940**: acquired by the Italian Government for conversion into a hospital ship. **September 1943**: seized at Spezia for hospital-ship service for Germany. **Mercy Mission**: 20

The *Aquileia* ex *Prins der Nederlanden* in hospital-ship livery. *Mario Cicogna*

With her hull painted black, Tirrenia Line's *Argentina* during a call at Valletta. *Michael Cassar*

ARGENTINA Tirrenia S.A. di Navigazione (Tirrenia Line)

5,526grt; 407.5ft LOA; 48ft beam
Russell, Port Glasgow (yard no. 582)
Triple-expansion steam reciprocating, twin screw

31 October 1907: maiden voyage Trieste–South America for Unione Austriaca di Navigazione S.A., Trieste, later Trieste–New York. **1919**: transferred to Cosulich Line. **1925**: transferred to Florio Soc. Italiana di Navigazione for trans-Mediterranean services. **1932**: owners became Tirrenia Flotte Riunite Florio-Citra. **December 1936**: owners became Tirrenia S.A. di Navigazione. **Mercy Missions**: 15 and 16

ARUNDEL CASTLE Union-Castle Line

19,118grt; 686ft LOA; 73ft beam
Harland & Wolff, Belfast (yard no. 455)
Steam turbine, twin screw

22 April 1921: maiden voyage Southampton–Cape Town; sister ship *Windsor Castle*. **1937**: taken in hand for modernisation with her sister – four original stick funnels replaced with two of broader, more modern style and bow raked, increasing overall length by 25ft. **1939**: considered for auxiliary employment as an Armed Merchant Cruiser but instead became a troopship. **Mercy Missions**: 25 and 26

The upgrade and modernisation she received in 1937 gave the *Arundel Castle* a more modern, even racy, look. *Richard de Kerbrech*

The *Asama Maru* of Nippon Yusen Kaisha. *Richard de Kerbrech*

ASAMA MARU Nippon Yusen Kaisha

16,947grt; 583ft LOA; 72ft beam
Mitsubishi, Nagasaki (yard no. 450)
Motorship, quadruple screw

10 October 1929: maiden voyage Yokohama–San Francisco; sister ship *Tatsuta Maru*. **1941**: taken up by the Japanese Government for conversion into an armed troop transport. **Mercy Mission**: 10

ATLANTIS ex Andes (1930) Royal Mail Line

15,135grt; 589ft LOA; 67ft beam
Harland & Wolff, Belfast (yard no. 434)
Triple-expansion steam reciprocating & LP steam turbine, triple screw

26 September 1913: maiden voyage Southampton–La Plata ports. **April 1914**: war service as auxiliary cruiser. **November 1919**: resumed South America service. **1930**: converted at Liverpool into white-hulled cruise ship *Atlantis*. **September 1939**: purchased by the British Government for conversion into Hospital Ship 33, managed by her former owners. **Mercy Missions**: 18 and 20

One of the earliest dedicated cruise ships, Royal Mail Line's *Atlantis*. *World Ship Society*

The *Miike Maru* in her Nippon Yusen Kaisha colours gives an impression of the intended appearance of the *Awa Maru*, one of her sister ships. *Nippon Yusen Kaisha*

AWA MARU Nippon Yusen Kaisha

11,249grt; 535ft LOA; 66ft beam
Mitsubishi, Nagasaki (yard no. 770)
Motorship, twin screw

24 August 1942: launched; intended for NYK's Kobe–Sydney service. **March 1943**: completed as an armed troop transport. **Mercy Mission**: 27

CABO DE BUENA ESPERANZA ex Maria del Carmen (1940) ex President Lincoln (1940) ex Hoosier State (1922) Ybarra Compania

14,187grt; 535ft LOA; 66ft beam
New York Shipbuilding Corp., Camden, New Jersey (yard no. 256)
Steam turbine, twin screw

September 1921: entered Orient service from San Francisco for the United States Shipping Board under charter to the Pacific Mail SS Co. **1925**: transferred to the Dollar Line, purchased outright. **1938**: owners became American President Lines. **1940**: sold to Berge & Co. **1940**: sold to Ybarra Compania for Barcelona–La Plata service. **Mercy Mission**: 24

A former American standard passenger-cargo ship, the *Cabo de Buena Esperanza* of the Ybarra Company. *Author's collection*

Built originally for Lloyd Triestino, the *Calitea* became an Adriatica Line ship in the late 1930s. *Mario Cicogna*

CALITEA Società Anonima Adriatica Navigazione (Adriatica Line)

4,013grt; 334ft LBP; 50ft beam
Cantieri Riuniti dell'Adriatico, Monfalcone (yard no. 1118)
Motorship, twin screw

October 1933: completed for Lloyd Triestino's Mediterranean service calling at Trieste, Venice, Fiume, Brindisi, Piraeus, Rhodes and Alexandria. **1936**: passed to Adriatica Line ownership, same route. **June 1940**: arrested at Malta by British Contraband Control along with the same company's *Rodi*. **Mercy Mission**: 1

CITTÀ DI TUNISI Tirrenia S.A. di Navigazione

5,419grt; 412ft LBP; 51ft beam
Cantieri del Tirreno, Riva Trigoso (yard no. 97)
Motorship, twin screw

May 1930: completed for Naples–Tripoli services via Palermo and Tunis or Catania, Syracuse and Malta of Florio Società Italiana di Navigazione; sister ship *Città di Napoli*. **1936**: owners became Tirrenia S.A. di Navigazione. **June 1940**: requisitioned and converted into an armed auxiliary cruiser, also transporting troops, supplies, fuel, vehicles and military equipment. **Mercy Missions**: 15 and 16

One of a number of similar motorships built between the wars for Florio Line that later passed to Tirrenia, the *Città di Tunisi*. *Author's collection*

Builders' trials view of the Ellerman Lines' *City of Canterbury*. *Ian Rae*

CITY OF CANTERBURY Ellerman City Line

8,421grt; 448.5ft LBP; 56.5ft beam
Swan Hunter & Wigham Richardson, Wallsend (yard no. 1189)
Quadruple-expansion steam reciprocating, single screw

February 1923: completed for London–India service. **1924**: transferred to Bombay–Durban–Cape Town–UK route. **1930**: returned to London–India service. **1939**: taken up for troopship duties. **Mercy Mission**: 11

CITY OF PARIS Ellerman City Line

10,902grt; 504ft LOA; 59.5ft beam
Swan Hunter & Wigham Richardson, Wallsend (yard no. 1129)
Steam turbine, single screw

February 1922: maiden voyage London–Far East ports, then entered the Ellerman City Line London–Bombay service. **1924**: cruises to northern capitals, then temporarily laid up before resuming London–India service. **1936**: London–Beira service via Cape Town. **September 1941**: requisitioned for war service as a troopship. **Mercy Mission**: 11

Another Swan Hunter-built Ellerman's ship, the *City of Paris*. *Ian Rae*

Second ship of the name, the *Conte Rosso* in Lloyd Triestino colours. She and her sister ship were built in Scotland by William Beardmore & Co. *Mario Cicogna*

CONTE ROSSO *Linee Triestine per l'Oriente – Oriens (Lloyd Triestino)*

17,856grt; 591ft LOA; 74ft beam
William Beardmore, Dalmuir, Glasgow (yard no. 611)
Steam turbine, twin screw

29 March 1922: maiden voyage Genoa–Buenos Aires for Lloyd Sabaudo. **15 May 1922**: Genoa–New York service. **1928**: resumed Genoa–La Plata ports service. **January 1932**: owners became Italia Flotte Riunite; immediately chartered to Lloyd Triestino for Trieste–Shanghai route via Suez. **December 1933**: transferred to Lloyd Triestino, same service plus trooping voyages to East Africa. **Mercy Mission**: 2

CONTE VERDE *Linee Triestine per l'Oriente – Oriens (Lloyd Triestino)*

18,765grt; 593ft LOA; 74ft beam
William Beardmore, Glasgow (yard no. 765)
Steam turbine, twin screw

21 April 1923: maiden voyage Genoa–Buenos Aires for Lloyd Sabaudo. **13 June 1923**: Genoa–New York service. **January 1932**: owners became Italia Flotte Riunite; Genoa–La Plata ports service. **5 October 1932**: chartered to Lloyd Triestino for Trieste–Shanghai route via Suez. **December 1933**: transferred to Lloyd Triestino. **3 June 1940**: laid up at Shanghai. **Mercy Mission**: 10

Lloyd Triestino's *Conte Verde*, sister ship of the *Conte Rosso*. Trapped at Shanghai from 1940, the *Conte Verde* was prevented from putting to sea for fear of capture by British warships believed to be waiting beyond the mouth of the River Yangtze. *Mario Cicogna*

After she transferred from the Vera Cruz and Colon routes, the *Cuba* was painted white for the West Indies service. *Jean-Yves Brouard collection*

CUBA *Compagnie Générale Transatlantique (French Line)*

11,337grt; 495ft LOA; 62ft beam
Swan Hunter & Wigham Richardson, Newcastle (yard no. 1108)
Steam turbine, twin screw

5 May 1923: maiden voyage St Nazaire–West Indies–Vera Cruz; later Vera Cruz service from Le Havre. **1930**: Le Havre–Colon service. **1935**: West Indies and 'Firm Coast' route (ports on the Caribbean coast and Gulf of Mexico). **31 October 1940**: intercepted by HMS *Moreton Bay* while en route from Martinique to Casablanca; confiscated by the Ministry of War Transport and transformed into a troopship under the management of Cunard White Star Line. **Mercy Mission**: 20

DINARD *Southern Railway*

2,291grt; 316ft LBP; 41ft beam
William Denny, Dumbarton (yard no. 1164)
Steam turbine, twin screw

July 1924: completed for the Southampton–Channel Islands night service. **October 1939**: taken over for conversion into Hospital Carrier 33. **Mercy Mission**: 5

The cross-Channel ferry *Dinard* of the Southern Railway Company. *R.H. Tunstall*

The *Djenné* at Brest on 18 April 1940 while serving as an armed transport. *Jean-Yves Brouard collection*

DJENNÉ Cie. de Navigation Paquet (Paquet Line)

8,790grt; 443ft LOA; 58ft beam
Forges et Chantiers de la Mediterranée, La Seyne (yard no. 1204)
Steam turbine, twin screw

June 1931: completed for Marseilles–Tangier–Casablanca service. **1939**: requisitioned at Toulon for conversion into an armed merchant cruiser. **April 1940**: supported Allied operations in Norway. **September 1941**: repatriated French troops from Syria and Lebanon to Marseilles. **February 1943**: seized and transferred to German control. **Mercy Mission**: 20

DROTTNINGHOLM ex Virginian (1920) Svenska Amerika Linien (Swedish America Line)

11,182grt; 538ft LOA; 60ft beam
Alexander Stephen, Glasgow (yard no. 405)
Steam turbine, triple screw

6 April 1905: maiden voyage Liverpool–St John's, Newfoundland for Allan Line, subsequently Liverpool–Montreal service; sister ship *Victorian*. **1917**: transferred to Canadian Pacific Line. **1920**: sold to Svenska Amerika Linien for Gothenburg–New York service. **March 1940**: laid up at Gothenburg. **Mercy Missions**: 8, 9, 20, 23, 25 and 28

Berthed at New York, the *Drottningholm. Swedish America Line*

DUILIO Lloyd Triestino

23,635grt; 635ft LOA; 76ft beam
Ansaldo, Sestri Ponente (yard no. 175)
Steam turbine, quadruple screw

30 October 1923: maiden voyage Genoa–New York for Navigazione Generale Italiana, later Naples–New York service. **August 1928**: Genoa–La Plata ports service. **January 1932**: transferred to Italia Flotta Riunite. **6 March 1934**: Genoa–Cape Town service via Suez and East Africa. **January 1937**: transferred to Lloyd Triestino; Genoa–Cape Town route via West Africa. **7 November 1939**: laid up at Genoa. **Mercy Missions**: 7, 12 and 17

EL NIL ex Tjerimai (1933) ex Wadai (1921) ex Marie (1917) ex Marie Woermann (1917) Khedivial Mail Steamship Co.

7,775grt; 426ft LBP; 56ft beam
Reiherstieg Schiffswerft, Hamburg (yard no. 463)
Quadruple-expansion steam reciprocating, twin screw

18 February 1916: launched as the *Marie Woermann* for the Woermann Line; laid up on completion. **1918**: acquired by the Deutsche Ost-Afrika Line for the Germany–Africa service. **28 August 1920**: entered service but immediately surrendered to the British Shipping Controller as a war prize. **1921**: awarded as reparation to Rotterdam Lloyd and placed on the Rotterdam–Malaya–Dutch East Indies service via Suez. **1932**: sold to the Societé 'Misr' de Navigation Maritime SAE (Khedivial Mail Steamship Co.) for the Alexandria–Naples–Genoa–Marseilles service. **1940**: chartered by the British Government for troopship service. **Mercy Mission**: 11

Berthed at the Prince's Landing Stage, Liverpool, the *Empress of Russia* of Canadian Pacific. *Author's collection*

EMPRESS OF RUSSIA Canadian Pacific Line

16,810grt; 592ft LOA; 68ft beam
Fairfield, Govan (yard no. 484)
Steam turbine, quadruple screw

1 April 1913: maiden voyage Liverpool–Hong Kong; subsequently Vancouver–Yokohama service; sister ship, *Empress of Asia*. **23 August 1914**: naval service as auxiliary cruiser. **12 February 1916**: resumed trans-Pacific service. **6 May 1918**: service as a troopship. **8 March 1919**: resumed trans-Pacific service. **28 November 1940**: requisitioned for troopship service for a second time. **Mercy Mission**: 20

GIULIO CESARE Lloyd Triestino

21,900grt; 634ft LOA; 76ft beam
Swan Hunter & Wigham Richardson, Newcastle (yard no. 967)
Steam turbine, quadruple screw

4 May 1922: maiden voyage Genoa–Buenos Aires for Navigazione Generale Italiana. **11 August 1922**: Genoa–New York service. **1925**: Genoa–La Plata ports service. **January 1932**: transferred to Italia Flotta Riunite. **4 February 1934**: Genoa–Marseilles–Gibraltar–Dakar–Cape Town service. **January 1937**: transferred to Lloyd Triestino. **20 April 1939**: Genoa–Shanghai service. **14 October 1939**: laid up at Genoa. **Mercy Missions**: 7, 12 and 17

Sporting her Italian Line livery, the *Giulio Cesare* at Marseilles in 1934. *Author's collection*

The *Gradisca* was originally the *Gelria* of Royal Holland Lloyd. *Mario Cicogna*

GRADISCA ex *Gelria (1935) Lloyd Triestino*

13,868grt; 560ft LOA; 65ft beam
Alexander Stephen, Glasgow (yard no. 454)
Quadruple-expansion steam reciprocating, twin screw

5 November 1913: maiden voyage Amsterdam–La Plata ports for NV Koninklijke Hollandsche Lloyd; sister ship *Tubantia*. **1935**: sold to the Italian Government, managed by Lloyd Triestino, employed part-time as a troopship and hospital ship. **June 1940**: full-time hospital ship. **Mercy Missions**: 6, 13, 14, 15, 16, 20 and 22

GRIPSHOLM *Svenska Amerika Linien*

18,134grt; 573ft LOA; 74.5ft beam
W.G. Armstrong, Whitworth, Newcastle (yard no. 999)
Motorship, twin screw

21 November 1925: maiden voyage Gothenburg–New York. **24 November 1939**: laid up at Gothenburg. **Mercy Missions**: 10, 19, 21, 22, 25 and 26

Swedish America Line's motorship *Gripsholm* in February 1934. *F.W. Hawks, courtesy of World Ship Society*

The *Kamakura Maru* showing the Japanese neutrality markings she carried between 1939 and 1941. Beyond her is the *Asama Maru. Richard de Kerbrech*

KAMAKURA MARU ex *Titibu Maru (1939)* ex *Chichibu Maru (1938)*
Nippon Yusen Kaisha

17,526grt; 584ft LOA; 74ft beam
Yokohama Dock Co., Yokohama (yard no. 170)
Motorship, twin screw

4 April 1930: maiden voyage Yokohama–San Francisco. **1938**: renamed following the adoption of a revised system of phonetic transliteration. **1939**: renamed again because of clumsy respelling of her new name. **December 1941**: converted into an armed troop transport with occasional interruptions for hospital-ship service. **Mercy Mission**: 11

LETITIA Donaldson Atlantic Line

13,475grt; 538ft LOA; 66ft beam
Fairfield, Govan (yard no. 601)
Steam turbine, twin screw

24 April 1925: maiden voyage Glasgow–Montreal for Anchor-Donaldson Line; subsequently Liverpool–Quebec–Montreal in summer months, Liverpool–Halifax, Nova Scotia–St John's, Newfoundland in the winter; sister ship *Athenia*. **9 September 1939**: taken in hand for conversion into an Armed Merchant Cruiser. **June 1941**: troopship duties until severely damaged. **1943**: repaired in the United States and simultaneously converted into Hospital Ship 66. **Mercy Mission**: 26

Sister ship of the *Athenia*, the first passenger liner sunk in the Second World War, the *Letitia* survived the war to become a MoT troopship. *World Ship Society*

The intermediate steamship *Llandovery Castle* served Cape Town via the Mediterranean, Suez Canal and East African ports. *Author's collection*

LLANDOVERY CASTLE Union-Castle Line

10,640grt; 487ft LOA; 62ft beam
Barclay, Curle, Glasgow (yard no. 606)
Quadruple-expansion steam reciprocating, twin screw

25 September 1926: completed for round-Africa intermediate service from London via the Mediterranean and Suez Canal; sister ship, *Llandaff Castle*. **1941**: commandeered for conversion into Hospital Ship 39. **Mercy Mission**: 6

MONARCH OF BERMUDA Furness Withy

22,424grt; 579ft LOA; 76.5ft beam
Vickers Armstrongs, High Walker (yard no.1)
Turbo-electric, quadruple screw

7 November 1931: completed for the so-called 'Millionaires Run' from New York–Hamilton, Bermuda; sister ship *Queen of Bermuda*. **November 1939**: converted into a troopship. **Mercy Mission**: 2

First of the so-called twin 'Millionaires Ships', the *Monarch of Bermuda. Author's collection*

The *Narkunda* with her sister *Naldera* sailed to either Australia or the Far East for P&O. This striking view shows her departing Tilbury in 1934. *Allan Green*

NARKUNDA P&O Line

16,227grt; 606ft LOA; 70ft beam
Harland & Wolff, Belfast (yard no. 471)
Quadruple-expansion steam reciprocating, twin screw

24 April 1920: maiden voyage London–Bombay, thereafter alternated between London–Bombay or London–Sydney, Australia routes; sister ship *Naldera*. **May 1940**: requisitioned for service as a troopship. **Mercy Mission**: 11

NEWFOUNDLAND Johnston Warren Line

6,791grt; 423ft LOA; 55ft beam
Vickers, Barrow (yard no. 617)
Quadruple-expansion steam reciprocating, twin screw

June 1925: completed for the Liverpool–St John's, Newfoundland–Halifax, Nova Scotia–Boston service; sister ship *Nova Scotia*. **7 September 1939**: requisitioned, later converted into Hospital Ship 38. **Mercy Mission**: 14

Johnston Warren Line's
Newfoundland at Liverpool.
B. & A. Feilden

The *Orduña* at
Liverpool on 25
August 1934. *World
Ship Society*

ORDUÑA Pacific Steam Navigation Co.

15,507grt; 569ft LOA; 67ft beam
Harland & Wolff, Belfast (yard no. 438)
Triple-expansion steam reciprocating & LP steam turbine, triple screw

19 February 1914: maiden voyage Liverpool–Rio de Janeiro–Montevideo–Valparaiso; after two round trips chartered by Cunard Line for the Liverpool–New York service. **April 1920**: resumed PSNCo.'s South America service. **May 1921**: Hamburg–Southampton–New York service under charter to Royal Mail Line. **1923**: purchased by Royal Mail. **1927**: returned to her original route for PSNCo. **1930**: Liverpool–Valparaiso via the Panama Canal. **Mercy Mission**: 2

PRESIDENT COOLIDGE American President Lines

21,936grt; 654ft LOA; 81ft beam
Newport News SB & DD Co, Newport News (yard no. 340)
Turbo-electric, twin screw

15 October 1931: maiden voyage New York–San Francisco–Far East for Dollar Line, subsequently San Francisco–Yokohama–Shanghai service; sister ship *President Hoover*. **1938**: owners became American President Lines. **15 July 1941**: converted into US Army troop transport. **Mercy Mission**: 4

The *President Coolidge* again, here painted in American President Lines livery. *American President Lines*

The *Rio Jachal* started her life as the *Campana* of Societé Générale de Transports Maritime (SGTM). *Jean-Yves Brouard collection*

RIO JÁCHAL ex Campana (1943) Argentine Government (Flota Mercante del Estado)

10,816grt; 527ft LOA; 67ft beam
Swan Hunter & Wigham Richardson, Newcastle (yard no. 1302)
Steam turbine, twin screw

December 1929: completed for the Marseilles–Buenos Aires service of Societé Générale de Transports Maritimes (SGTM); sister ship *Florida*. **1940**: laid up at Buenos Aires. **28 July 1943**: seized by the Argentine Government and placed under the management of Flota Mercante del Estado. **Mercy Mission**: 24

ST JULIEN Great Western Railway

1,885grt; 291.5ft LOA; 42.5ft beam
John Brown, Clydebank (yard no. 509)
Steam turbine, twin screw

May 1925: completed for Weymouth–Channel Islands service; sister ferry *St Helier*. **1927–28**: aft, dummy funnel removed during winter refit. **9 September 1939**: engaged carrying troops of the British Expeditionary Force to France. **5 October 1939**: converted into Hospital Carrier 29. **Mercy Mission**: 5

Great Western Railway's *St Julien* was completed with two funnels. The aft-most, a dummy, was removed in 1927. *Maritime Photo Library*

Italia Line's *Saturnia* was originally built with sister ship *Vulcania* for the Austrian company Cosulich. The angled top to her funnel was added post-war. *Antonio Scrimali*

SATURNIA Italia Line

24,470grt; 632ft LOA; 79.5ft beam
Cantieri Navale Triestino, Monfalcone (yard no. 160)
Motorship, twin screw

21 September 1927: maiden voyage Trieste–La Plata ports for Cosulich Line. **1 February 1928**: Trieste–New York service. **January 1932**: integrated into Italia Flotta Riunite. **8 May 1935**: used as troop transport to East Africa. **August 1936**: resumed Trieste–New York service. **June 1940**: laid up at Trieste. **Mercy Missions**: 7, 12 and 17

SINAIA Fabre Line

8,567grt; 439.5ft LBP; 56ft beam
Barclay, Curle, Glasgow (yard no. 583)
Triple-expansion steam reciprocating, twin screw

25 September 1924: maiden voyage Marseilles–New York. **1940**: taken up for war service. **September 1941**: repatriated French troops from Syria and Lebanon to Marseilles. **1942**: seized by Germans at Marseilles. **1943**: converted into a hospital ship. **Mercy Mission**: 20

The *Sinaia* of Compagnie Cyprien Fabre. Her sister ship was the *De La Salle* of the French Line. *Author's collection*

TAIREA British India Line

7,933grt; 465ft LOA; 60ft beam
Barclay, Curle, Glasgow (yard no. 595)
Triple-expansion steam reciprocating, twin screw

5 May 1924: after a positioning maiden voyage entered the Apcar service, Calcutta–Rangoon–Penang–Singapore–Hong Kong–Amoy–Shanghai–Moji–Kobe. **1937**: Bombay–Durban service. **1940**: converted into Hospital Ship 35. **Mercy Missions**: 14, 15, 16 and 20

TALAMBA British India Line

8,018grt; 466ft LOA; 60ft beam
Hawthorn, Leslie & Co, Newcastle (yard no. 533)
Triple-expansion steam reciprocating, twin screw

2 October 1924: entered Apcar service. **1939/1940**: converted into Hospital Ship 43. **Mercy Missions**: 14, 15 and 16

Sister ship of the *Tairea*, this is the *Talamba*. The third sister was the *Takliwa*. *Maritime Photo Library*

The *Talma*, another British India Line passenger ship. With sister ship *Tilawa*, they, like the *Tairea* trio, had limited accommodation for around 130 passengers maximum. *Author's collection*

TALMA British India Line

10,005grt; 471ft LOA; 59ft beam
Hawthorn, Leslie & Co, Newcastle (yard no. 529)
Quadruple-expansion steam reciprocating, single screw

13 September 1923: maiden voyage India–Japan, Apcar service. **December 1939**: requisitioned as a personnel carrier; later troopship service. **Mercy Mission**: 13

TATUTA MARU ex Tatsuta Maru (1938) Nippon Yusen Kaisha

16,975grt; 584ft LOA; 72ft beam
Mitsubishi, Nagasaki (yard no. 451)
Motorship, quadruple screw

25 April 1930: maiden voyage Yokohama–San Francisco. **1938**: name modified following the adoption of a revised system of phonetic transliteration. **1941**: taken up for conversion into an armed troop transport. **Mercy Missions**: 4 and 11

Nippon Yusen Kaisha's *Tatsuta Maru*, sister ship of the *Asama Maru*, had her name truncated to *Tatuta Maru* from 1938. *Nippon Yusen Kaisha*

The Japanese transport *Teia Maru* started out as the *Aramis*, the first of three sister ships that, unusually, had squat box-like funnels – an inelegant style that was adopted for other ships of the Messageries Maritimes fleet. The *Aramis* is seen here at Saigon. *Author's collection*

TEIA MARU ex Aramis (1942) Japanese Government

17,537grt; 566ft LOA; 69.5ft beam
Forges et Chantiers de la Mediterranée, La Seyne (yard no. 1206)
Motorship, twin screw

21 October 1932: maiden voyage Marseilles–Far East for Messageries Maritimes. **1939**: fitted out as an auxiliary cruiser at Saigon. **April 1942**: seized by the Japanese at Saigon. **2 June 1942**: entered service after conversion into armed troop transport. **Mercy Mission**: 19

VULCANIA Italia Line

24,469grt; 632ft LOA; 79.5ft beam
Cantieri Navale Triestino, Monfalcone (yard no. 161)
Motorship, twin screw

19 December 1928: maiden voyage Trieste–New York for Cosulich Line. **January 1932**: integrated into Italia Flotta Riunite. **2 February 1935**: used as troop transport to East Africa. **21 December 1935**: resumed Trieste–New York service. **1941**: used as troop transport Taranto–Tripoli, then laid up at Trieste. **Mercy Missions**: 7, 12 and 17

Caught in mid-conversion from ocean liner to troop transport, the *West Point* ex *America* photographed on 2 June 1941. *US Naval Historical Center*

The Italia liner *Vulcania*. *Paolo Valenti*

WEST POINT ex America (1941) United States Lines

26,454grt (US measurement); 723ft LOA; 93.5ft beam
Newport News SB & DD Co, Newport News (yard no. 369)
Steam turbine, twin screw

10 August 1940: cruise New York–West Indies – had been intended to enter New York–Southampton–Le Havre–Hamburg service but prevented by the war in Europe. **June 1941**: taken up for auxiliary service with the US Navy. **Mercy Mission**: 3

Repatriation Transfer Ships

CABO DE HORNOS ex Maria Pipa (1940) ex President Wilson (1940) ex Empire State (1922) Ybarra Compania

12,597grt; 535ft LOA; 65.5ft beam
New York Shipbuilding Corp., Camden, New Jersey (yard no. 254)
Steam turbine, twin screw

June 1921: entered Orient service from San Francisco for the United States Shipping Board under charter to the Pacific Mail SS Co. **1925**: transferred to the Dollar Line and purchased outright. **1927**: round-the-world service, New York–Hawaii–Far East–Mediterranean–New York. **1938**: owners became American President Lines. **1940**: sold to Berge & Co. **1940**: sold to Ybarra Compania for Barcelona–La Plata service. **Mercy Mission**: 24

DEUTSCHLAND Deutsche Reichsbahn

2,972grt; 356ft LOA; 51ft beam
Stettiner Vulcan, Stettin-Bredow (yard no. 292)
Triple-expansion steam reciprocating, twin screw

June 1909: completed for the Sassnitz–Trelleborg train ferry service for Koniglich Preussische Eisenbahn Verwaltung; sister ferry *Preussen*. Owners later became Deutsche Reichsbahn. **1940**: believed to have been renamed *Stralsund* but this cannot be confirmed. **19 October 1942**: struck a mine off Trelleborg; repaired at Malmö. **14 March 1943**: returned to service. **Mercy Missions**: 20 and 25

The Baltic train ferry *Deutschland*, introduced on the Sassnitz–Trelleborg route in 1909. *Deutsches Schiffahrtsmuseum*

The Swedish train ferry *Drottning Victoria*, which worked in conjunction with her sister vessel *Konung Gustav V*, and the German flag pair *Deutschland* and *Preussen*. *Author's collection*

DROTTNING VICTORIA Svenska Statens Järnvägar, Trelleborg

3,074grt; 371.5ft LOA; 50ft beam
Swan Hunter & Wigham Richardson, Low Walker (yard no. 802)
Triple-expansion steam reciprocating, twin screw

June 1909: completed for Trelleborg–Sassnitz train ferry service; sister ferry *Konung Gustav V*. **1939**: requisitioned by Swedish Navy for service as an auxiliary minelayer. **1940**: returned to her owners. **Mercy Missions**: 20 and 25; 28 not confirmed

METEOR [II] ex Rostock (1942) ex Meteor (1940) Det Bergenske D/S

3,717grt; 346ft LBP; 44ft beam
Blohm & Voss, Steinwerder, Hamburg (yard no. 170)
Triple-expansion steam reciprocating, twin screw

28 May 1904: completed as a specialist cruise ship for Hamburg Amerika Line. **August 1914**: served as naval accommodation ship. **May 1919**: ceded to Great Britain as a war prize; operated on behalf of the Shipping Controller by Royal Mail Line. **March 1921**: purchased by Bergen Line for cruising. **27 July 1940**: seized at Bergen following Germany's invasion of Norway; converted into a naval hospital ship. **1942**: apparently renamed *Meteor II* although the name on the ship's hull remained as *Meteor*. **Mercy Missions**: 20 and 25

The small Bergen Line cruise ship *Meteor*. *Bjørn Milde*

The *Oranje*, here seen in her hospital-ship colours, did not complete a single round voyage for the Nederland Line before the outbreak of war. After reaching Batavia (now Djakarta) on her maiden voyage, she was prematurely laid up at Surabaya for her security. *Author's collection*

ORANJE Nederland Line

20,017grt; 656ft LOA; 83.5ft beam
Nederlandsche Schps. Maats., Amsterdam (yard no. 270)
Motorship, twin screw

4 August 1939: cruise Amsterdam–Madeira. **4 September 1939**: maiden voyage Amsterdam–Batavia, Dutch East Indies, via Suez. **December 1939**: laid up at Sourabaya. **February 1941**: moved to Sydney to be fitted out as a hospital ship. **30 July 1941**: entered service as Hospital Ship D1; served with the Royal Australian Navy but under the Dutch flag and manned by a Dutch crew. **Mercy Mission**: 20

RÜGEN Stettin-Riga Steamship Co. (Rud Christ Griebel)

2,170grt; 313ft LOA; 38ft beam
Stettiner Oderwerke, Stettin-Grabow (yard no. 644)
Triple-expansion steam reciprocating, twin screw

20 May 1914: completed for the Stettin, Swinemünde and Rügen coastal excursion service for the Stettin Steamship Co. (J.F. Braeunlich). **21 November 1914**: taken over for service as an auxiliary minelayer. **14 March 1919**: ceded to Great Britain as a war prize but not delivered to UK. **17 April 1919**: purchased from Shipping Controller, London, by her original owners. **1921**: operation taken over by Stettin-Riga Steamship Co.; transferred to Stettin–Riga–Tallinn–Helsinki service. **25 September 1939**: converted into a naval hospital ship. **Mercy Missions**: 20 and 25

Stettin-Riga Steamship Co.'s (R.C. Griebel) elegant Baltic steamer *Rügen*. *Deutsches Schiffahrtsmuseum*

VALAYA Thai Navigation Company

1,311grt; 224ft LBP; 36ft beam
Hong Kong & Whampoa Dockyard, Kowloon (yard no. 550)
Triple-expansion steam reciprocating, single screw

June 1918: completed for coastal services around Thailand and South East Asia for Siam Steam Navigation Co., a subsidiary of the East Asiatic Company of Denmark; sister ship *Suddhadib*. **1941**: appropriated by Thai Government and transferred to Thai Navigation Company. **1942**: used to carry cargo and fuel for Japanese Army. **Mercy Mission**: 10; 11 not confirmed

Ships Engaged in Other Wartime Humanitarian Operations

KARSKÄR Stockholms Rederi A/B Svea

582grt; 208.5ft LOA; 31.5ft beam
Öresundsvarvet, Landskrona (yard no. 78)
Motorship, single screw

6 April 1943: completed for Baltic cargo service of Svea Line. **Mercy Mission**: 30

KASTELHOLM Svenska Amerika Linien

891grt; 180.5ft LBP; 30.5ft beam
Eriksberg, Gothenburg (yard no. 228)
Triple-expansion steam reciprocating, single screw

February 1929: completed for Swedish America Line's Östersjön–Gothenburg feeder service. **Mercy Mission**: 30

KRONPRINSESSAN INGRID Rederi A/B Goteborg-Frederikshavn Linjen (Trapp)

794grt; 210.5ft LOA; 36ft beam
Frederikshavn Vaerft, Frederikshavn, Denmark (yard no. 204)
Motorship, twin screw

11 June 1936: completed for Gothenburg–Frederikshavn coastal service. **Mercy Mission**: 30

LILLIE MATTHIESSEN ex Imperator (1933) Sven Salén Rederiana

983grt; 231.5ft LOA; 33ft beam
Stavanger Stoberi & Dok, Stavanger (yard no. 48)
Triple-expansion steam reciprocating, single screw

1905: completed for D/S A/S Svithun of Stavanger; operated under charter to the United Fruit Company. **1933**: sold to Rederi A/B Westindia (Sven Salén) of Stockholm. **Mercy Mission** 29

MAGDALENA ex Nora (1939) ex Langdon (1914) Sven Salén Rederiana

1,262grt; 236ft LBP; 32ft beam
Readhead, South Shields (yard no. 179)
Compound-expansion steam reciprocating, single screw

March 1882: completed for J. Fenwick & Sons for general cargo service based on north-east coast of UK. **1914**: sold to Otto Banck. **1939**: sold to Sven Salén. **Mercy Mission**: 29

PRINS CARL ex Munin (1940) Swedish Navy

1,262grt; 264ft LBP; 37.5ft beam
Finnboda AB, Nacka (yard no. 315)
Triple-expansion steam reciprocating, single screw

October 1931: completed for North Sea service of Stockholms Rederi A/B Svea. **1940**: sold to Swedish Navy for conversion into a hospital ship. **1944**: converted into a naval radar training ship. **Mercy Mission**: 30

RÖNNSKÄR Stockholms Rederi A/B Svea

582grt; 208.5ft LOA; 31.5ft beam
Öresundsvarvet, Landskrona (yard no. 79)
Motorship, single screw

22 September 1943: completed for Baltic cargo service of Svea Line. **Mercy Mission**: 30

2

THE MERCY MISSIONS

Although the ICRC, through its role bestowed by the Geneva Convention and in the many initiatives it unilaterally pursued on behalf of prisoner victims, was central to the global repatriation efforts of the Second World War, as stated earlier not all repatriation missions were conducted under the auspices of that organisation or necessarily according to Convention rules. While all these operations followed the same general principles, a number were undoubtedly organised independently through the Protecting Powers or by the Detaining Powers alone via other third party government legations. This would appear to be especially true of some of the exchange operations conducted early on in the conflict, as they do not feature in any of the reports or other documentation of the ICRC pertaining to its wartime activities. The immediate concern of the ICRC on the outbreak of war was the repatriation of sick and wounded military prisoners and, whereas it expressed a desire for civilian detainees to be treated in a like fashion, initially it was not itself able to implement those wishes in practice.

Irrespective of whether or not the ICRC was instrumental in initiating or arranging certain prisoner or diplomat exchanges, all known mercy missions that took place between September 1939 and September 1945 are related in this section.

Ship Colour Schemes

To avoid repetition, because they apply to more than one mercy mission, all the descriptions of the colour schemes adopted for those ships that engaged in wartime repatriation voyages are provided here. There are only a very few ships whose colouring is unknown or uncertain, but some can be speculated on with reasonable certainty.

Hospital Ships

In accordance with the protocols laid down in Article 5 of the Hague Convention, hospital ships were required to be clearly marked and illuminated, exploiting what was called 'the distinctive emblem' – the Red Cross. This comprised white colouring over all surfaces of the entire ship, including the funnels, with the Red Cross emblem prominently displayed on either side of the hull and each funnel. Running along the length of each of the ship's sides was a broad band or stripe, a minimum of 4ft in depth, connecting the Red Cross symbols. This was painted green when the ship was operated by a belligerent country or red if the ship was operated under charter from a neutral country or a medical agency. These colours were retained for repatriation duties. In this book, the following ships were painted in hospital-ship livery: *Aquileia, Atlantis, Dinard, Gradisca, Letitia, Llandovery Castle, Meteor, Newfoundland, Oranje, Rügen, St Julien, Sinaia, Tairea* and *Talamba*.

Cartel Ships

The ships taken up for repatriation missions under cartel arrangements were painted in a diversity of colour schemes. Some of them, but by no means all, featured the cross emblem, mostly in a colour other than red, to symbolise the association, if not direct link, with the Red Cross organisation and the humanitarian nature of their business. While there were many schemes adopted for these ships, they can be loosely grouped together with their minor differences highlighted.

British Ship Colour Schemes

Excluding the hospital ships, the biggest group of mercy ships was the British cartel ships, and the painting of these ships followed a fairly standardised pattern. Broadly speaking, they were painted grey overall, either a darker or lighter shade, with the Union Jack flag displayed prominently on the sides of their hulls. In most cases, fore and aft on the hull were rectangular patches, comprising three vertical stripes in red, white and blue – similar to the French national flag. In addition, some, but again not all, carried a legend in bold 4ft-high letters on their sides, in most cases immediately above the Union Jack. This general scheme was applied to the *Arundel Castle, City of Canterbury, City of Paris, Cuba, El Nil, Empress of Russia, Narkunda* and *Talma*, with the following variations:

The *Arundel Castle* had the legend 'PROTECTED' in white characters on a black rectangular background, whereas on the *Cuba* the same legend was painted directly onto her grey hull and was positioned aft of the Union Jack.

The *City of Canterbury* and *City of Paris* had the legend 'DIPLOMATIC'.

The *El Nil* had the legend 'DIPLOMAT' and her funnel had red, white and blue bands painted on it. Her upper works were yellow above a black hull.

The *Narkunda* had black tops to her grey funnels. It is not definite that either the *Empress of Russia* or *Narkunda* had any legend painted on their sides, while the *Talma* displayed her name in large white letters possibly in addition to one of the noted legends.

The colour schemes of the *Monarch of Bermuda* and *Orduña* have not been discovered and it is possible that they retained plain navy grey colouring alone although, if so, it is not clear how they achieved safe-passage between Liverpool and Lisbon without some visual indication of their purpose.

Italian Ship Colour Schemes

On the Axis side, Italy contributed eight vessels to repatriation missions. Apart from a particular group of four, none of the other Italian ships were painted the same. The *Città di Tunisi* was painted overall in a light shade, either white or very pale grey, with the legend 'PROTECTED' painted in big white letters, much larger than on any other ship at almost two decks high. For contrast on her light hull, the legend was painted over a black rectangular patch.

In contrast, the *Conte Rosso*, which retained her commercial colours along with the Italian flag from the neutrality markings worn between September 1939 and June 1940, had the legend 'DIPLOMAT' in very small black characters enclosed by parentheses.

The *Argentina* had 'PROTECTED' in white letters painted over camouflage colours, while the *Calitea* may well have still been in her commercial colours, as her mission took place at an early stage of the conflict with Italy, though this cannot be confirmed.

The remaining four Italian ships – *Duilio*, *Giulio Cesare*, *Saturnia* and *Vulcania* – which were engaged for three mercy voyages to East Africa, were painted identically. All their vertical and horizontal surfaces were painted white, and also their funnels. Overpainted on the sides of their hulls were two red crosses with between them, amidships, the Italian national flag. There were no coloured bands or stripes along their sides, revealing that they were not hospital ships. Another difference was the treatment of their funnels. These had a central blue disc on which was painted a prominent white cross.

Japanese Ship Colour Schemes

Japan's six mercy ships, one of which was a chartered Italian liner, fell into two groups as far as their colouring schemes were concerned.

The *Asama Maru*, *Tatuta Maru* and the chartered *Conte Verde* all had black hulls and white upper works. Along each side of their hulls there were four evenly spaced white crosses with amidships, between the two innermost crosses, the Japanese national flag. There was also a small red cross on the upper works above the flag. Funnels were all black with a white cross on either side.

The *Awa Maru*, the *Kamakura Maru* and the *Teia Maru* were completely different. They were painted dark sea-green overall with large white crosses on their sides, their funnels and, for aerial recognition, on their hatch covers and above the bridge. Most other mercy ships also carried protective markings on their decks or hatch covers for the same reason.

Swedish, French and German Ship Colour Schemes

The two best-known wartime mercy ships, the *Drottningholm* and *Gripsholm*, essentially carried their owners' commercial colours throughout the war, along with their Swedish neutrality markings. These comprised, on the hull, the Swedish flag, the word 'SVERIGE' and the ship's name in bold letters, and patches of vertical blue and yellow stripes fore and aft. It is possible that, while operating services across the Baltic, the train ferry *Drottning Victoria* was painted likewise. However, while they were engaged on mercy voyages, the *Drottningholm* and *Gripsholm* also carried an additional legend. For the *Gripsholm*, this was 'DIPLOMAT', which she carried throughout all the missions she undertook. On the *Drottningholm*, though, it changed according to the nation by which she was chartered. For the US Government it was 'DIPLOMAT', for the British it was 'PROTECTED' and, towards the end of the war when she was chartered by Germany, it was 'FREIGELEIT' aft, which translates as 'safe-conduct' or 'safe-passage', and 'PROTECTED' forward.

The former French liner *Djenné*, while in German hands, had a unique and distinctive paint scheme. When she arrived at Barcelona in November 1943, her general colouring was dark grey, both on her hull and superstructure as well as her funnels. On the sides of her hull, towards the bow and stern, were red swastika symbols in white discs and the symbols rotated at approximately 45 degrees from upright. Between the Nazi emblems, in large letters she also carried the legend 'FREIGELEIT'.

The colour scheme of the German train ferry *Deutschland*, which shuttled across the Baltic with the *Drottning Victoria*, is unknown.

Other Ship Colour Schemes

The *Rio Jachal*, a French ship seized by Argentina, which sailed with the *Cabo de Buena Esperanza*, chartered from Spain, had a particularly busy paint scheme. Her name and her port of registry, Buenos Aires, featured repeatedly along her hull, interspersed with the blue-and-white Argentine flag. Centrally she displayed the legend 'DIPLOMATICOS' with 'REPUBLICA ARGENTINA' beneath it.

Although it cannot be confirmed, both the *Cabo de Buena Esperanza* and *Cabo Hornos* probably carried Spanish neutrality colours, the former sailing under warrant clearance with the possible addition of 'DIPLOMATICOS' on her hull.

The adoption of the German language for the *Djenné* in the legend declaring her protected status, and later that of the *Drottningholm*, is a matter of curiosity, as was the Argentine use of 'DIPLOMATICOS', but there appear to have been no rules that stipulated the exclusive use of English in these circumstances.

As is the case for the *Deutschland*, it has not been possible either to determine how the small coastal steamer *Valaya*, which ferried repatriates from Bangkok to Saigon, was painted.

Despite the fact that the United States had not entered the war in June 1941, the *West Point* had by then relinquished the neutrality markings and commercial colours she had carried as the *America*. Photographs from the time when she crossed the Atlantic on her mercy mission to Lisbon show her painted troopship grey overall in accordance with the prevailing US Navy directives. Most probably this would have been the official concealment scheme Measure 1 – Dark Grey System introduced for application from January 1941.

The *President Coolidge*, waiting in Shanghai around the same time for the instruction to sail to Japan on a similar mission, was probably also painted in either Measure 1 or Measure 3 – Light Grey System, introduced around the same time, as she had been taken up as a US Army transport from 15 July 1941.

—◦◦◦—

The missions that follow are laid out in chronological sequence, some grouped together where appropriate. It should be noted that the numbers appended to each mission are unique to this book and are there simply to provide a convenient cross-reference tool as well as a link to the ships listed in Chapter 1.

In the descriptions of categories of repatriates, the word 'British' is for the most part generic, applying also to Commonwealth persons from the Dominions of Australia, Canada and New Zealand and the colonies of the Empire, besides those from the British Isles. In the same way, for 'Allied', read American, British, Dutch etc.

Mission 1: Valletta, Malta, June 1940

Almost certainly, the first safe-passage repatriations of the Second World War occurred in connection with Italy's declaration of war on the British Empire on 10 June 1940. Of these, the very first involved the Italian passenger ship *Calitea* in an event that is recalled quite differently from the perspective of Italian and

Maltese historians. British documentation of this episode, though limited, sheds more light on the facts and reveals both valid elements and inaccuracies in these opposing views. For interest, both versions of the events are related here along with the details from the official British records.

Rightly, Italian accounts describe the *Calitea* as the 'first Italian protected ship of the Second World War'. Apparently, after having been held in Valletta for three days – by inference three days after the declaration of war – the *Calitea* sailed for Syracuse, Sicily, on 13 June, with over 600 Italian subjects, accompanied by a British minesweeper. The repatriation had been organised, it is claimed, on the insistence of the local Italian Regal Consul, General Mario Canino, but with the full blessing of the Maltese Governor, General Sir William Dobbie, despite objections from the British Government in London. One harsh critic in Great Britain, it is claimed, was said to have complained that Dobbie's concession amounted to 'allowing the prey to escape'. After being escorted by the minesweeper through the safe channel, it was only a short distance, approximately 125 miles, to the port of disembarkation, and the *Calitea* would have arrived there later on the day of her departure or during 14 June 1940.

With a soldier on guard at her bow, it is thought this view of the *Calitea* probably dates from after June 1940. *Mario Cicogna*

Maltese recollections, as substantiated by the Heritage Malta War Museum, are somewhat different, asserting that the ship's departure occurred on 10 June 1940, just before Italy declared war. The *Calitea*, it is affirmed, along with another Italian ship, the *Rodi*, had been seized by British Contraband Control in Maltese waters and escorted into Valletta, though the date when this occurred is not stated. Vivian de Garay, Malta's Commissioner of Police from 1955 to 1971, takes up the story in the serialised *Malta at War*, edited by John A. Mizzi:

> My duties as CID inspector included port control, passports and exit permits. On 10 June 1940 [on the request of the then Commissioner of Police], I delivered a message from Colonel Ede, in charge of security, to the Consul for Italy. After carrying out the Commissioner's orders, I proceeded to the Customs House in Valletta where some 300 Italian subjects were awaiting repatriation to Italy.
>
> The expatriates were to be put onboard an Italian passenger boat, one of two which had been seized by Contraband Control and brought into harbour. Colonel Ede told me that the British subjects married to Italian citizens would be allowed to remain in Malta with their children if they so wished. He also urged me to expedite matters because officially the war would start at midnight and there was a possibility of air raids during the coming night [in fact the first bombs fell on Malta on 11 June]. Some of the Italians onboard [the *Calitea*] were in a state of panic and a Royal Navy officer went onboard to reassure them all that the authorities were guaranteeing them safe-conduct and that they would be put ashore at Syracuse unharmed.
>
> On that occasion, I remember, an Italian in civilian suit went up to the officer and said, 'You have behaved like a gentleman and I would like to return the compliment. I would like to confess that I am a serviceman.' He was then led off the boat.
>
> On the afternoon of 11 June [after the *Calitea* had departed] I was detailed to provide an escort for a car load of Italians who were being taken to Fort Salvatore at Vittoriosa where a number of Maltese internees were also being held. The Italians had been crew members on one of the two ships, *Colitea* and *Città de Rodi* [sic], which had been seized by Contraband Control.

The few records held in the National Archives, Kew, reveal that the material facts are to some extent at variance with both the Italian and Maltese recollections. The various communications on this subject show that the Italians asserted that the *Calitea* had in effect been snatched with the *Rodi*, the implication being illegally, on the pretext that she would make a convenient means of conveying Italian aliens from Malta. Although, in the event, she *was* used for this purpose, the ship had in fact been detained by Contraband Control purely for inspection purposes on the orders of the Admiralty, the interception and arrest of the *Calitea* and *Rodi* having occurred on 9 June.

It is evident, too, from correspondence between the Italian Consul and the Brazilian Ambassador in London, who was representing Italian interests, that a more general, reciprocal evacuation of British and Italian diplomatic personnel (Mission 2) was simultaneously under consideration by the two governments. There was an implied threat that this could be jeopardised if the *Calitea* was not released and allowed to proceed. The *Calitea* did finally depart Valletta on 13 June – loaded with repatriates – but only after the British Government signified its approval for the Italian Consul General and his party, which included his wife, to board the ship.

The suggestion that General Sir William Dobbie engaged in an unapproved repatriation – the Italians dubbed it 'fai da te' (do it yourself), implying Dobbie acted unilaterally – is refuted by the content of his telegram of 11 June to SECER, Chapelries, London (presumably the Admiralty), in which it is evident his declared intention to use the *Calitea* as the means of transportation would only have been with the Admiralty's approval and consent. On such a vulnerable island with only a small British military garrison to protect it, Dobbie was clearly anxious to have potentially disruptive Italians out and the sooner the better, though with London's approval. Dobbie's telegram also reveals that there were around 700 Italian men and women awaiting either repatriation aboard the *Calitea* or, should their return not be permitted, internment on the island.

As for the *Rodi*, taken as a war prize and allocated to the Ministry of War Transport, she continued to Palestine via Egypt a month later under her new identity of *Empire Patrol*, arriving on 22 July 1940 with the 157 Jewish refugees from Poland who had boarded her in Trieste.

Missions 2A and 2B: Lisbon, June and July 1940

Concurrent with the short repatriation voyage of the *Calitea*, the British and Italian governments were indeed arranging another, more formalised and larger scale, repatriation exchange through the neutral Portuguese port of Lisbon. Three ships were involved: the liners *Conte Rosso*, *Monarch of Bermuda* and *Orduña*.

Historical accounts suggest that there was a single exchange of British and Italian diplomats, their staff and families, as well as some French nationals who, in the wake of the capitulation of France, desired to return home. In reality, though, the dates of the movements of the two British ships do not support this conjecture, the only conclusion being that two exchanges took place and that the *Conte Rosso* sailed to and from Lisbon twice rather than once.

Her first departure, from Ancona with British consular officials who had travelled from Durazzo, Albania, via Bari, was to have been on or about 12 June, well before the first exchange took place. She may have been delayed, though, because the *Monarch of Bermuda* – the first of the British ships which had been due to leave the Clyde on 14 June – had been held up, unable to secure a full crew. When the *Monarch of Bermuda* finally left Glasgow on 21 June 1940 she had 600 Italians on board including the Italian Ambassador. Thirty others declined to join the ship at the last minute and were interned. She sailed direct to Lisbon following precise navigational instructions and arrived there three days later.

The transfer of passengers between her and the *Conte Rosso* occupied three more days. The *Monarch of Bermuda* then commenced her return voyage on

The *Monarch of Bermuda* as a troopship heading for Gibraltar in 1945. *Grant Bailey*

The *Conte Rosso* as a mercy ship. It is not known whether this photograph of her was taken at Lisbon or at an Italian port. *Mario Cicogna*

ORDUNA
28·6·47

The *Orduña* making a call at Valletta on 28 June 1947. Although she was still in Government service, her peacetime colours have been restored. *Michael Cassar*

27 June, arriving back in the River Clyde, where her passengers disembarked, on 30 June 1940. It is conceivable that the *Conte Rosso* may have returned to Civitavecchia on Italy's west coast, as she is also recorded as transporting the staff of the British Embassy in Rome, probably on the second run to Portugal.

To conclude the operation, the *Orduña* sailed from Liverpool on 19 July 1940 and, just as the *Monarch of Bermuda* had done, she proceeded unescorted direct to Lisbon along a 'special route', protected by international safe-conduct guarantees. She arrived on 25 July and, during the next six days, the rendezvous was made with the *Conte Rosso* and the second batch of repatriates exchanged. The *Orduña* sailed on her return voyage on 31 July and arrived back at Liverpool on 4 August 1940 from where, on the termination of her special mission, she was directed to Valparaiso for the resumption of her former duties. For her part, the *Conte Rosso* arrived back in Italy on 30 July.

The numbers of persons exchanged on these voyages is not known, but it is understood that an equal number travelled in each direction. Given the size and peacetime complements of the three ships, their total passengers could have been of the order of 1,000 moving in each direction. The fact that two exchanges were necessary tends to support this assumption.

The Italians subsequently complained that their citizens had not been treated appropriately, either during their brief internment in Great Britain or during the sea crossing. The British, for their part, suspected the Italians of having had a submarine secretly concealed beneath the *Conte Rosso*, necessitating an intensification of Royal Navy security patrols when she passed through the Strait of Gibraltar.

It appears evident that the ICRC played no part in this affair. The United States, as Britain's Protecting Power, almost certainly did, but whatever arrangements were made with Germany to ensure immunity from attack for the *Monarch of Bermuda* and *Orduña* cannot now be determined.

Mission 3: Lisbon, July 1941

Prior to the United States' entry into the Second World War, efforts were intensified to extricate American citizens from Europe and the Far East, in particular from Japan. In September 1939, the Special Division of the State Department was created to facilitate the return of American nationals from war zones, either real or potential. Ultimately, the division would also be responsible for repatriation missions during hostilities.

In the summer of 1941, the United States was still a neutral country, but preparations for imminent conflict had been stepped up and measures were being taken to get the country into a state of war preparedness by accelerating armaments and shipbuilding programmes and the requisitioning of commercial ships for conversion into naval auxiliaries. As part of this, the United States Lines' new flagship *America* was taken over as a troop transport in June 1941 to become the USS *West Point*.

Two years earlier, when war broke out in Europe, the *America*'s United States Lines' fleetmates *Manhattan* and *Washington* had been employed evacuating

The *West Point* on 15 June 1941, just weeks prior to her repatriation mission to Lisbon. *US Naval Historical Center*

Americans while still working the last of their scheduled service passages. In order to continue with the repatriation of civilians from the summer of 1941, the United States was obliged to negotiate and arrange a formal exchange agreement with Germany. This was an unusual situation that did not not accord with any of the rules normally applicable to such missions, either under the articles of the Geneva Convention (because no prisoners of war were involved) or established cartel practices (because at the time the two countries were not adversaries). No doubt endorsement of the arrangement and the safe-passage guarantee for the *West Point* – the only ship deployed for an exchange mission – was readily extended by the British Government. However, it would seem that, having lost her commercial colours and neutrality markings with their inherent protection under a coat of navy grey, she was displaying no physical decorative features to indicate her protected status.

After embarking 137 Italian and 327 German diplomats, she departed New York on 16 July 1941, heading straight to Lisbon where she docked on 23 July at the end of her very first Atlantic crossing. In the meantime, 321 American and sixty-seven Chinese diplomats were taken by train across France and Spain to the Portuguese capital, where the physical exchange took place the day after the *West Point*'s arrival. Two days later, the *West Point* departed on the return leg of her special mission and by 1 August 1941 she was back in New York. Thus ended her brief employment as a mercy ship, for she was immediately routed to Halifax, Nova Scotia, from where, attached to Convoy WS12X, she conveyed British troops to the Middle East via South Africa.

Mission 4A, 4B and 4C: Kobe, August 1941; San Francisco and Los Angeles, October and December 1941

A parallel mercy mission to that of the *West Point* was attempted by the United States with Japan, but ultimately this failed. However, the corresponding missions organised by the Japanese were more successful.

Unlike the Lisbon operation, in which aliens were carried out and national citizens were brought home by the same ship, the intention in the proposals with Japan essentially centred around two ships, one American and the other Japanese, each to call at the other's territory to simultaneously collect their own nationals for repatriation. Amid difficult negotiations, the simultaneous element became an encumbrance that could not easily be achieved and it was soon discarded.

At the time, August 1941, the American President Lines' ocean liner *President Coolidge*, already taken up by the US Army for transport duties, was at Shanghai. She was ordered to remain there pending a hoped-for positive outcome to the negotiations after which she was to proceed to Kobe on her part of the exchange.

The problem was that in the souring relations between the two countries in the run-up to war, exacerbated by the US Government's freezing of Japanese national assets, each side imposed increasingly onerous restrictions on those wishing to leave, limiting the personal assets and funds they could take with them. The Japanese suggested that it could relax its regulations if America was also to liberalise its exit rules, but in the prevailing hostile climate that was not going to happen.

When Japan did agree to the intended repatriation call of the *President Coolidge*, despite all the ensuing difficulties, it nevertheless imposed other conditions. The *President Coolidge* was to go to Yokohama rather than Kobe, she was not to enter the Inland Sea and was permitted only to collect official government employees. This was unacceptable to America, which questioned why – besides diplomats, consular officials and civil servants – private citizens could not also be permitted to board the ship. Without assurances to that effect and because the *President Coolidge* could not be kept waiting indefinitely at Shanghai, the mission – or at least the American part – was abandoned and the ship ordered to return directly to the United States taking only those repatriates collected from China. Despite that, Japan's endeavours to proceed with repatriation runs of its own continued unabated and the first took place that October. The Nippon Yusen Kaisha (NYK) liner *Tatuta Maru*, earmarked to undertake the mercy trip, was requisitioned as a charter vessel. Under radio silence, which was maintained throughout the entire voyage, she sailed from Yokohama on 15 October with American and Canadian passengers. She called at Honolulu (23–24 October 1941) and arrived at San Francisco on 30 October. After exchanging her passengers for returning Japanese she sailed the same day. In a return call at Honolulu on 2 November more Japanese were embarked, the voyage ending at Yokohama on 14 November.

The schedule for a proposed second voyage by the *Tatuta Maru* was then communicated to Secretary of State, Cordell Hull, by the Japanese Ambassador, Admiral Kichisaburō Nomura. She would leave Yokohama on 2 December to arrive via Honolulu at Los Angeles on 14 December and San Francisco two days later. After picking up her Japanese passengers, she would proceed to South American ports to collect more would-be repatriates, at Manzanillo, Mexico, on 19 December and Balboa in the Canal Zone on 27 December. She would then return to Japan.

Japan's infamous surprise attack on Pearl Harbor on 7 December 1941 rendered the whole mercy exercise as redundant, but in reality the second voyage of the *Tatuta Maru* had been no more than a carefully contrived subterfuge. On her departure, her master had been officially notified that after four days he would receive a special communication, which he was to act upon immediately. When it reached the ship at midnight on 6 December, the message ordered him to turn the *Tatuta Maru* around and return her to Japan.

The *Tatuta Maru* in neutrality colours. *US Maritime Commission*

The Americans, despite their expectation that war would erupt at any time, took the *Tatuta Maru*'s itinerary at face value and notified the Japanese early on 7 December that it too intended to send a repatriation ship, the *President Madison*, to Chingwangtao to collect some US Marines and 615 civilians from areas north of Peking (now Beijing). Whether or not that exercise transpired is unknown but the *Tatuta Maru*'s spurious voyage ended back at Yokohama on 14 December 1941 and three days later she was under the command of the Imperial Japanese Navy.

Mission 5: Dieppe, October 1941

In the spirit of its declared intentions, the ICRC took the initiative in July 1940 in opening negotiations with Germany and Great Britain for the establishment of a ferry service between the two countries as a method for the repatriation of the seriously wounded and sick. Negotiations for the actual repatriation were dealt with by Switzerland in its capacity as a Protecting Power. Proposals aimed at implementing such a POW exchange mechanism were communicated to both governments, suggesting initially that the ICRC itself would acquire and make available a ship to operate under the Red Cross emblem, plying across the English Channel, the proviso being that the costs must be shared equally between the two belligerents. In the event, it was unable to charter anything suitable.

Germany's response was to counter-propose that it would supply a hospital ship of its own for this purpose, but that half the running costs should be borne by Great Britain. For its part, the British Government stated a preference for an ICRC-chartered vessel and, further, presented outline conditions that it stipulated should be adopted as the basis for operating such a service.

Nothing had been agreed, but the reactions, at least, had been positive. However, some four months were to pass with nothing definite arranged until the United States, acting as Protecting Power for the British, advised the ICRC that Germany had withdrawn its support for the initiative on the grounds that the English Channel was no longer a safe sea area. Nonetheless, the seeds of a deal had been sown and, rather than abandon the concept entirely, Great Britain offered to prepare a new proposal.

Time dragged on until, in February 1941, the Swedish Red Cross stepped in, offering to run an exchange operation across the North Sea for seriously sick and wounded prisoners, provided it had the blessing of the two adversaries. The ICRC, anxious to keep things moving, gave its support to the Swedish plan and, accordingly, entered into negotiations with the British and German authorities. Ultimately, although it is not clear how, the British hospital carriers *Dinard* and *St Julien*, both short-sea ferries, were selected and accepted for what would have been the first Anglo-German exchange – the 'Daylight Truce' or 'Exchange Truce' scheme, as it was dubbed.

Dieppe was selected as the port at which the physical exchange would take place, the passage to and from France to be along the 'Channel Truce Lane' or 'Neutrality Lane', as it was described, the tentative date of the exchange set for Saturday to Sunday, 4–5 October 1941. Haggling now proceeded as to who was to qualify for repatriation and in what numbers. Meanwhile, the *Dinard*

Hospital Carrier 28, the *Dinard*, photographed at Gourock. *Lt S.J. Bendall, Crown Copyright*

and *St Julien* were moved to Newhaven in preparation for the mission – the former from Belfast, the latter from Aberdeen – first to Southampton, where she received repairs, before proceeding along the Channel coast. Simultaneously, 103 qualifying German POW, as identified and agreed upon, were transferred by train over various routes to Newhaven docks where they boarded the *Dinard*. They were joined by Red Cross nurses and RAMC personnel selected to care for the sick and injured servicemen en route.

It was at this point that everything began to unravel, largely because of German intransigence and its repeated insistence on complicated adjustments to the conditions of the operation. Initially, the intention had been to exchange only fifty German POW for 1,600 British in accordance with the Geneva Convention rules of 'without regard to rank or numbers'; that is, without equivalence. Germany, though, wanted to modify the arrangements, firstly by including women and children internees, to which Britain reluctantly agreed. Accordingly, sixty German female internees were taken from Port Erin, Isle of Man, via London to Newhaven and embarked aboard the *St Julien* on the understanding that a reciprocal number of British women interned in Germany would be returned. Next, Germany wanted to include merchant seamen in the exchange, whose status was still debatable, but the final straw was its demand upon absolute parity in numbers. Despite the extent to which the preparations had advanced, with Germans already waiting aboard the ships at Newhaven and requiring complicated security measures to allow them to exercise, and 1,150 British POW already entrained from the Reich aboard a Swiss hospital train and held pending final transfer in a holding centre in Rouen, the British authorities were unwilling to accede to these belated demands.

The *St Julien*, Hospital Carrier 29. With the *Dinard*, she would have completed the first Anglo-German exchange had unreasonable demands not caused it to be aborted at the last moment. *Newall Dunn collection*

Consequently, the mission was abandoned, the men and women returned to their camps and the *Dinard* and *St Julien* released for other duties on 9 October – the former to Falmouth and subsequently to the River Clyde, and the latter returning to Southampton for more repairs from 10 October 1941.

Inevitably, there were recriminations on both sides, made worse in the UK because a lot of pre-publicity had been allowed. The national dailies following the story carried the collapsed exchange as front-page news. Perhaps the worst consequence of the failed mission was that it altogether undermined efforts to repatriate prisoners and it would be two years before a successful Anglo-German exchange would occur.

Mission 6: Smyrna (now Izmir), April 1942

Although the prospect of repatriations of any kind between Germany and Britain had receded for the foreseeable future, a more pragmatic atmosphere characterised the dealings between Britain and Italy with regard to setting up exchanges, both countries keen to repatriate their sick and wounded servicemen.

During the Eighth Army's successes in North Africa, over 100,000 Italian prisoners who had become both a logistical and humanitarian liability were taken, particularly those who were seriously sick and wounded. Though the numbers concerned would be relatively small compared with the movements of quantities of healthy prisoners by troopship to prison camps in the UK and Canada – a highly dangerous process, as highlighted by the loss of the troopship *Laconia* in September 1942 – a better option was available for the sick and wounded by organising exchanges for equivalent British POW held in Italy. Such a proposal was made by the British Government, insisting that any such exchange should be performed strictly in accordance with the relevant articles of the Geneva Convention. This was accepted and, working through American and Brazilian diplomatic channels, agreement was reached by 12 January 1942, whereby a first repatriation would take place on 8 April 1942 at Smyrna in Turkey, thanks to the accommodation of the Turkish authorities.

The ICRC was informed and requested to provide delegates to accompany each group of returning prisoners, along with the ICRC representative in Ankara who would also travel to the port to assist in the supervision of the actual exchange. In the event, as the first cautiously approached but generally successful repatriation exercise, it proved to be the catalyst for a series of Anglo-Italian exchange missions from April 1942 to September 1943.

For the first exchange, two hospital ships were deployed: the *Gradisca* representing the Italians and the *Llandovery Castle* for the British interests.

When the *Laconia* was sunk on 12 September 1942 she was carrying 1,793 deported Italian prisoners of whom almost three-quarters lost their lives. *Author's collection*

The *Gradisca* left Naples, where she had been based, sailing to Bari where she embarked 128 British POW. From there, she headed alone to Smyrna. Meanwhile, the *Llandovery Castle* departed Alexandria on 5 April 1942 with 919 Italian POW, arriving in Smyrna two days later. It should be noted that these POW figures do not accord with the numbers reported in ICRC-1948 of sixty and 340 respectively. There are two possible explanations for this. It is quite probable that the higher counts include protected personnel added to the POW, but it is also known that there were differences between planned and actual numbers. Certainly for ships of the size and capacity employed, prisoner numbers of sixty and 340 would have been extremely low.

The exchange completed, the *Gradisca* returned to Bari and the *Llandovery Castle*, which sailed on the day after the exchange, reached Alexandria on 11 April 1942 where waiting medical teams organised the onward transportation of the sick and injured by train to Cairo. The entire scene was captured on film and reported in newspaper articles by journalists and cameramen covering the disembarkation.

Although it was suspected that the Italians had not entirely honoured the spirit of the agreement, by excluding some of those servicemen who had been passed by its Mixed Medical Commission, this did not prevent or hamper future exchanges.

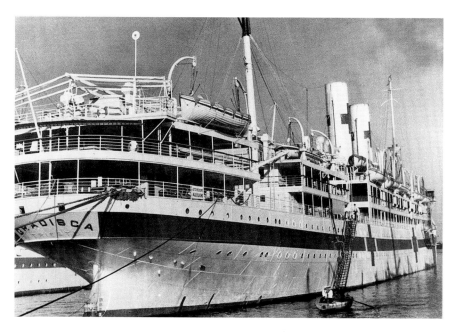

The first Anglo-Italian exchange was performed by the Italian hospital ship *Gradisca*. *Mario Cicogna*

The British *Llandovery Castle*, Hospital Ship 39, seen here arriving at Alexandria in 1942, possibly at the time of the Smyrna exchange. *Philip J. Heydon, Crown Copyright*

Mission 7: Berbera, April 1942

Just as in the North African campaign, large numbers of Italian prisoners were also taken during the fighting in East Africa in the former Italian colonies of Somaliland, Ethiopia and Eritrea. The difference in this region, when it was secured by British forces, was that the local population of Italian colonial civilians was also rounded-up and interned, many of them in large camps at Asmara. It presented the occupying authorities with a quite different set of concerns, managing so many non-military persons in custody. Not only did they have to be sheltered, fed and, where necessary, treated medically, it soon became apparent that there was also a great deal of animosity towards these civilian internees from the native population from which they needed to be protected. Intent on reprisals, it was feared there could be a massacre if the Italian captives remained in the camps. To prevent this, the need to move them away, ideally by repatriation to Italy, became a matter of urgency. Essentially, Britain also wanted to be rid of those who were no more than a drain on limited resources, along with those who were disruptive within the internment camps.

Instigated by the British and aided and supported by the US, Swedish and Swiss governments, the latter through the Special Division of its London Legation, a relief operation, unofficially dubbed Operation *Guano*, was sought to alleviate these concerns. In what were probably the only one-sided repatriations during the Second World War (that is, repatriations without a reciprocal exchange), an agreement was negotiated with the Italian Government whereby four Italian ocean liners would be permitted, under strict conditions, to proceed to ports on the East African coast to convey the interned civilians back to their homeland.

The mercy voyages that had so far gone ahead had been over relatively short distances, even the Atlantic crossing of the *West Point*. The four Italian ships, in contrast, would be making a round trip of some 25,000 miles. During this voyage they would need to take on fresh water, essential lubricants and top up their bunkers regularly. Fuel presented the greatest concern – Britain wanted to ensure the ships had sufficient fuel to complete their mercy mission, but not an excess in reserve that might find its way into Italian warships or be put to some other military use.

As part of the agreement, Britain permitted an Italian oil tanker to collect fuel supplies for the repatriation ships from Aruba in the Netherlands West Indies (Netherlands Antilles until October 2010) and take it to Las Palmas and St Vincent in the Cape Verde Islands, this peripheral dimension of the operation equally under its watchful eye. An acute British concern was that the Italians, taking advantage of the opportunity, might try to intercept the tanker and divert it to a neutral or Vichy port.

The tanker selected to collect the oil – the 7,291grt *Lucania*, a British-built ship dating from 1902 and owned by Ditta Luigi Pittaluga Vapori – was, however, prevented from completing her particular assignment. She was torpedoed, set on fire and sunk by the British submarine HMS *Una* on 12 February 1942 off Crotone in the position 39.20N, 17.25E while en route from Taranto to Genoa. This was despite the fact that she had been painted in special colours for her protected status, as stipulated in the negotiations – a black hull with the national flag prominently displayed centrally on her sides, plus white discs on the hull and funnel. Clearly, there had been a breakdown of communication in the British chain of command. The authorities in Rome protested in the strongest terms, but they did not allow the unfortunate incident to prevent the continuation of the mercy programme. The *Lucania* was replaced by two other oil tankers, the 6,349grt *Arcola* and the 4,799grt *Taigete*, one for diesel oil and the other for furnace oil. Perhaps as an additional safeguard, the *Arcola* and *Taigete*, though manned by an Italian crew like the *Lucania*, also carried British officers and an armed Royal Navy guard. Without further incident, they eventually arrived at Curaçao, much to the amazement of some observers. A *Time* magazine correspondent expressed it perfectly: 'What were Italian ships doing, picking up Allied oil in the Netherlands West Indies? The answer was as unusual as the sight.'

Fuel stocks were also organised for other replenishment points for the homeward voyage, the oil and other stores supplied to the four liners to be paid for in gold through banks in nominated neutral countries. For replenishment at Berbera in British Somaliland (now Somalia), the ships' destination, bunker fuel was delivered from Aden by the tankers *British Genius* and *British Chancellor*, while water was conveyed from Safaga aboard the tanker *Hermes*. All three ships were protected by safe-conduct guarantees, in accordance with which they were required to be repainted in a distinctive colour scheme. This comprised a blue cross on a large white background (rectangle) on each side of the funnel, on the deck and on the ships' sides, fore and aft. For nighttime recognition they were to have a large illuminated white cross on each side of the upper works and one facing aft.

With the fuelling arrangements made, the first of three planned mercy voyages could get underway. By this time, the four Italian liners were fully prepared and ready to go. In the conversion of the motorships *Saturnia* and *Vulcania*, some of the accommodation spaces had been adapted as dormitories and it was probably the same on the steamships *Duilio* and *Giulio Cesare*. For the purposes of the repatriation, planning was based on a capacity for 2,517 persons on each of the motorships and 2,310 on each turbine steamer.

On 4 April 1942, the *Vulcania* sailed from Genoa and the *Saturnia* from Trieste. Two days later, south of the Balearics, they rendezvoused 20 miles from Majorca and proceeded together to Gibraltar, their first call, where they arrived on 7 April. The *Duilio* and *Giulio Cesare* also sailed from Trieste some three to four days later. Already aboard the *Vulcania* was the former Governor of Italian Somaliland, Francesco Saverio Caroselli, supervising the mission on behalf of the Italian

Government. He was joined by a British commission, while Senior British Naval Officers (SBNO) and armed parties went aboard each of the liners.

On each ship, too, the radio room was secured under British control. The frequencies to be used, the ships' call signs and the timings of communications and other rules, including the use, when necessary, of the British and Allied Merchant Ship (BAMS) cipher, were assigned by the British authorities. Each day's noon position was to be transmitted in plain language. As was deemed appropriate, radio traffic with the Italian authorities would be routed via Coltano wireless station, near Pisa.

The *Saturnia* and *Vulcania* sailed from Gibraltar on 8 April 1942 and then proceeded along the route assigned by the Admiralty, calling at St Vincent (11–13 April) to take on food, fuel and water, and arriving at Port Elizabeth on 24 April for further bunkering and replenishment of stores. Meanwhile, the *Duilio* and *Giulio Cesare* arrived at Gibraltar on 11 April, sailed the next day, bunkered at Las Palmas and arrived at Port Elizabeth four days after the first pair.

When they sailed again, all four ships made for Berbera, the *Saturnia* and *Vulcania*, arriving there on 5 May. The turbine pair were held up at Port Elizabeth because the Sperry gyro-compass aboard the *Giulio Cesare* was out of action, requiring repairs to its commutator and armature.

The *Saturnia* at Gibraltar in 1942 on the first mission to Italy's former East African colonies. *Mario Cicogna*

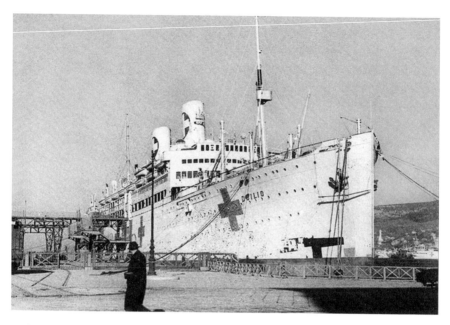

Undergoing conversion at Trieste, the Italian mercy ship *Duilio*. In the distant background to the right is the *Saturnia*, also undergoing preparation for the first East African repatriation voyage. *Paolo Valenti*

The *Giulio Cesare* in her special ICRC mercy mission livery. *Crown Copyright*

It had been estimated that the physical embarkation of repatriates at Berbera would take from two to three weeks, a matter of some concern because it was the start of the monsoon season, threatening the most unfavourable conditions. The original plan had been for the ships to bunker for the return voyage prior to boarding, but with inclement weather threatened and the tankers not due to arrive from Aden until 15 May, it was decided to commence embarkation first, starting 7 May. As it turned out, the boarding of repatriates was performed faster than expected and, by 13 May, the *Saturnia* and *Vulcania* were loaded, fuelled and ready to leave, waiting only for water to arrive from Egypt. The Italian Government requested that they be permitted to call at Tanga in Tanganyika (now Tanzania) on the return voyage to collect Italians waiting there, but this was refused by the British Admiralty.

The *Vulcania* was first to leave Berbera, on 16 May, followed by the *Saturnia* on 17 May and the *Duilio* and *Giulio Cesare* on 24 May. The run back to the Mediterranean retraced the outbound route. The *Saturnia* and *Vulcania*, reunited at sea, called at Port Elizabeth (27–28 May), Las Palmas, Gibraltar (18 June, to disembark the British officials, radio operators and naval party), Naples (21–22 June), Livorno (23 June) and Genoa, where they arrived on 24 June 1942. Following behind them, the *Duilio* and *Giulio Cesare* reached Port Elizabeth on 5 June, called at Las Palmas, Gibraltar (24 June), Naples (27–28 June) and Livorno (29 June), arriving at Genoa the same day. Safe-conduct protection for all four ships was extended to forty-eight hours after they docked at Genoa to provide for secure disembarkation.

Following final disembarkation, disinfection and cleaning, a period of lay-up for the four ships followed, pending the launch of the second East African voyage anticipated for October that year. It is of interest to note that while Britain guaranteed the safe passage of the four Italian liners, both Berlin and Tokyo opposed the agreement and declared that they would not honour their protected status. This presented a real risk to the operation, given the knowledge that U-boats were present in the South Atlantic and Japanese submarines were patrolling the Indian Ocean.

The total number of repatriates conveyed from East Africa to Italy in this first mission was 9,376. The complements of the ships comprised 2,489 on the *Saturnia* (1,128 women, 1,157 children and 204 men), 2,403 on the *Vulcania* (1,154 women, 1,055 children and 194 men), 2,287 on the *Duilio* (1,235 women, 862 children and 190 men) and 2,197 on the *Giulio Cesare* (1,001 women, 816 children and 380 men). Despite some initial uncertainty, even a measure of anxiety, the mission had gone smoothly. The only difficulty that had been encountered occurred at Berbera when the Vichy Government complained that some of the passengers had crossed through French Somaliland without permission, the proposed remedy being that 150 French civilians should be included among the repatriates on the second voyage.

The *Vulcania* at Naples on 21 June 1942, at the end of the first East African mercy mission.
Mario Cicogna

Missions 8 and 9: Lisbon, May and June 1942

Whereas the attempts to exchange either prisoners or civilians between Germany and Great Britain had stalled, the United States was able to reach agreement with Germany on the mutual exchange of diplomats and internees and implement it within six months of its entry into the war.

It was considered by that time that few ex-patriot Americans remained in Europe and that it would be possible, with a suitable ship, to have the residue brought home in no more than two voyages. Conversely, a vast number of enemy aliens had by then been interned in the United States, their numbers swollen through arrangements that had been concluded with various South American and Latin American nations, arising from which aliens from those countries were deported mainly aboard American ships to holding camps in the United States pending possible repatriation. Many ships found themselves engaged in this trade, among them Moore-McCormack's 'Good Neighbour Trio' as they were called, the *Brasil*, *Argentina* and *Uruguay*. Several ships from America's coastwise passenger fleet were also employed on deportation voyages, such as the *Acadia*, *Evangeline*, *Florida*, *Iriquois*, *Madison* and *Shawnee*. There was even a former German liner, the

Orinoco, which had been arrested at Vera Cruz, Mexico, and returned to service under the Mexican flag as the *Puebla*.

When it became known that the neutral Swedish ship *Drottningholm*, then laid up at Gothenburg, was available for charter, the US State Department's Special Division launched negotiations via the Swiss and Swedish governments to acquire it. By 4 March 1942, a deal had been struck and two months later, on 1 May 1942, the *Drottningholm*, fully prepared for her charter role, sailed for New York

She arrived on 6 May 1942 and within twenty-four hours she had embarked 948 Axis aliens, both diplomats and internees, who, besides the USA, had come from several American republics. The majority of them were of German extraction, but also among them there were Italians, Bulgarians and Hungarians. They were joined by five US Government officials who were to oversee the operation.

Six days later, US diplomatic personnel and civilian internees held in Germany departed for Lisbon by train where they arrived on 14 May. The *Drottningholm* reached Portugal two days later and had turned round, following completion of the exchange by 22 May, a swift operation with little ceremony. The precise numbers of returning American civilians is not known, but it is probable that it would have been comparable to the quantity of outbound passengers.

Back in New York by 30 May 1942, the *Drottningholm* immediately prepared for another repatriation run. She sailed on 3 June and had returned with the final consignment of returning citizens from the Americas by 30 June 1942. Again, the passenger figures are unknown, but it can be assumed that they were similar to those on the first voyage.

Sporting the legend 'DIPLOMAT', indicating that she was under charter to the United States, the *Drottningholm* is seen at New York with the skyscrapers of Manhattan Island in the background. *World Ship Society*

After disembarkation, the services of the *Drottningholm* were dispensed with and there were no more exclusively US–German civilian exchanges as such after that date. The *Drottningholm*, though, was subsequently taken up under charter by the British Government, becoming known over the next three years together with her fleetmate *Gripsholm* as the most celebrated of the mercy ships of the 1939–45 conflict.

Mission 10: Lourenço Marques, July 1942

The United States also made faster progress than Great Britain with regard to instigating repatriations with the Japanese. As early as 13 December 1941, just one week after the onset of hostilities, a request was made via the Swiss Embassy in Tokyo for consideration to be given to an exchange of interned diplomatic personnel and civilians.

Bearing in mind the obstacles that had been encountered while attempting to arrange such a process before the eruption of war, this was a bold and optimistic appeal. Contrary to expectations, it received a positive response. The Japanese made it clear they were never going to endorse the exchange of wounded and sick prisoners, but, mindful of the plight of thousands of their fellow countrymen and Japanese-Americans interned in the United States, they were ready to support the conclusion of an exchange agreement for civilians, which they announced on 5 January 1942, declaring their intention to guarantee safe passage for the ships that would need to be committed.

Inevitably, there were contentious issues that had to be resolved, principal among them the Japanese insistence on absolute reciprocity, driven by an acute sensitivity to what it perceived to be unequal treatment in international affairs. There was a dispute over the amount of money each repatriate could take with them, finally settled at $300 for each American and 1,000 Yen for each Japanese citizen. Even the question of who would porter luggage from the quayside onto the ships presented problems – for the Japanese, it would have meant serious loss of face to carry enemy baggage. Ultimately, all the details were settled and the operation was ready to be launched.

For this expedition the Americans had chartered the larger Swedish America liner *Gripsholm*, which had been laid up at Gothenburg until May 1942, placing her under the management of American Export Lines. Her extra space was required to carry the anticipated 1,500 passengers travelling in either direction; also her greater bunker and stores capacity were vital. This would be a significantly longer voyage, with calls at Rio de Janeiro out and back. It is understood that, already bedecked in her special livery, she made the voyage to New York under safe-passage provisions, carrying 194 US citizens who had been stranded in various Scandinavian countries.

Prior to her requisition as a Japanese transport ship, the *Asama Maru* was painted in neutrality colours. *Author's collection*

For their part, the Japanese allocated the former trans–Pacific liner *Asama Maru* and chartered the *Conte Verde*, then lying at Shanghai, from the Italian Government. It is reported that the latter ship was renamed *Teikyo Maru* for the mission, but there was no evidence of any such change on the ship's hull.

Preparations for the exchange involved some localised movement of the ships prior to the official departure. The *Asama Maru* went first from Nagasaki to Kobe, where Latin American diplomats boarded her, and from there to Yokohama. Commencing on 13 June she was repainted and prepared internally. Four days later, American diplomatic personnel were embarked, including the US Ambassador from Tokyo, Joseph Grew, along with his staff and their families. At this point there was a delay while the final details of the exchange were thrashed out. For the next eight days the *Asama Maru* rode at anchor off Kisarazu, in Tokyo Bay, waiting for the green light permitting her to proceed to Shanghai.

Meanwhile, the *Conte Verde* had left Shanghai for Nagasaki on 7 June before continuing to Osaka seven days later. By 21 June she was back in Shanghai where she was given her new coat of paint and commenced boarding her passengers. Among them was the American Consul General in China, Frank Lockhart. On 26 June, the *Asama Maru* briefly joined her there before sailing again the next day.

Across the world, the final preparations were also being made for the *Gripsholm's* departure. On 17 June she embarked a total of 1,083 Japanese and Siamese diplomats, including the Japanese Ambassador to the United States, Kichisaburo

Nomura, and the former Japanese Ambassador to Germany, Kurusu Saburō. A large number of internees were also taken aboard. The next day she departed for Brazil. At Rio de Janeiro, another 417 passengers were embarked, among them the Japanese Ambassador and embassy staff, and the *Gripsholm* then set out across the South Atlantic for Lourenço Marques (now Maputo), the selected neutral exchange port in Portuguese East Africa (now Mozambique).

The Japanese part of the mission required calls to be made at more ports en route to pick up listed repatriates distributed across China and South East Asia. From Shanghai the *Asama Maru* made first for Hong Kong where she embarked another 377 passengers – American, Canadian and other nationality consular staff, missionaries and private citizens – to add to the 430 she was already carrying. On 30 June she sailed, arriving next at Saigon (now Ho Chi Minh City) where a further 114 repatriates were embarked. Many of this group of internees had been brought to Saigon aboard the small passenger steamship *Valaya* of the Siam Navigation Company (an East Asiatic Company subsidiary) on an unscheduled voyage around the coast from Bangkok. By this time the *Asama Maru* was carrying 921 exchange passengers.

From Saigon, the *Asama Maru* continued to Singapore. She arrived on 6 July, meeting the *Conte Verde*, which, having left Shanghai on 29 June, had sailed direct to Singapore with a passenger complement that numbered some 600. The *Conte Verde* had been the focus of some unwelcome attention on the run down from Shanghai. One day, she had been spotted, brightly illuminated, some 4 miles distant by the American submarine USS *Plunger*. Having received the safe-passage clearance instruction from COMSUBPAC (Commander Submarine Force US Pacific Fleet), the submarine took no action other than to observe the liner and take a photograph of her as she passed half a mile away off the starboard beam.

Among the repatriates who boarded the *Asama Maru* and *Conte Verde* at Saigon were a group brought from Bangkok aboard the *Valaya*, which operated from the East Asiatic Company quay, Bangkok. *Willy Brorson*

A rare photograph showing the *Conte Verde* while under charter to Japan as a mercy ship. *Paolo Valenti*

Neither of the two Japanese mercy ships docked at Singapore, but they took on fuel, fresh water and supplies while at anchor before making their crossing of the Indian Ocean. A small number of additional passengers also embarked, bringing the total to around 1,600, not quite the equivalence that the Japanese had demanded for the exchange. Of course, these figures are imprecise and may not be absolutely correct either, as they vary from record to record; in fact, some records have contradictory counts. Nonetheless, whatever the precise numbers were, split almost equally between embassy and consular staff and civilian internees, the Japanese appear to have been happy with the balance.

From Singapore, the *Asama Maru* and *Conte Verde* departed together on 9 July, passing through the Sunda Strait and entering the Indian Ocean in tandem, the *Asama Maru* leading the way. At Lourenço Marques on 22 July, they docked wide apart on the main deep-water quay. When the *Gripsholm* arrived later the same day, she took the vacant berth between the other two ships.

The physical exchange took place on 23 July and lasted just four hours. First the Japanese personnel aboard the *Gripsholm* disembarked, each one carefully counted and checked-off on the lists provided by either party. Next around 7,000 Red Cross parcels were transferred to the Japanese ships. Finally, the Allied passengers descended to the dockside and, in orderly queues from either direction, made their way to the *Gripsholm* and boarded her at the bow and stern.

Despite the speed of the actual exchange, the three ships remained in port for a few more days, no doubt bunkering and replenishing their stores for the

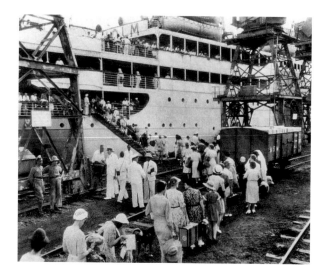

American and other nationality internees board the *Gripsholm* at Lourenço Marques prior to departure for home. *Author's collection*

Berthed at New York, the 'diplomat' ship *Gripsholm*. *US Navy*

return voyage. The *Asama Maru* and *Conte Verde* departed on 26 July, reached Singapore (9–11 August) and arrived at Tateyama on 19 August. They entered Yokohama the following day, the final destination for the *Asama Maru*, which was swiftly returned to naval duties. For the *Conte Verde*, however, the charter and, possibly, her safe-passage clearance extended back to Shanghai. After sixteen days at Yokohama she left for Shanghai, returning to her anchorage in the Huangpo River on 8 September 1942.

The *Gripsholm*'s return voyage retraced the outward route. Lourenço Marques was left on 28 July and, after dropping off Brazilian officials and civilians at Rio de Janeiro on 16 August, she arrived back in the Hudson on 25 August 1942, docking in New Jersey.

The entire operation had run smoothly and there had been few incidents or irritations that could have undermined subsequent repatriations planned for under the US-Japanese exchange agreement. Nonetheless, it would be October 1943 before the follow-on mission took place.

Mission 11: Lourenço Marques, September 1942

Within two months of the first US-Japanese exchange, a repatriation mission between the British and Japanese was arranged, also to take place at Lourenço Marques in two phases. Representing three of the nations fighting with the British forces – Australia, India and New Zealand – besides Great Britain herself, this mission was considerably more complex than the American operation.

No fewer than six ships were committed to the overall operation, making voyages from Melbourne and Fremantle, Bombay (now Mumbai), Liverpool and Yokohama. They were the *City of Canterbury*, *City of Paris*, *El Nil*, *Narkunda*, *Kamakura Maru* and *Tatuta Maru*. The Siam Steam Navigation steamship *Valaya* or her sister *Suddhadib* may also have been engaged as previously in a repeat of the transfer from Bangkok to Saigon, for some 104 persons were transferred from Thailand to join the *Tatuta Maru*. Whereas the *Valaya* is specifically named in the US-Japanese mission, no identities are recorded for the Anglo-Japanese exchange.

Triggered by a Swiss proposal lodged with both parties in February 1942, negotiations commenced to determine who was to be repatriated, the numbers in each case and the routes to be followed under safe-passage protection. It was then a question of assembling the required tonnage and preparing them for their respective passages.

Even before the US-Japanese exchange had taken place, a start was made in repositioning the British vessels and getting them painted in recognised protective colour schemes in readiness for the anticipated mission. On 28 June 1942, the *City of Canterbury* was moved from Bombay to Colombo where she was taken in hand by dockyard workers. Twelve days after her arrival she sailed on 13 July for Melbourne, arriving there on 4 August.

On 30 July, three more ships set out from their base ports: the *El Nil* from Liverpool, the *Tatuta Maru* from Yokohama and the *Narkunda* from Greenock. The *El Nil*'s departure was beset by hiccups, first because her safe-passage clearance had not been confirmed by either Germany or Italy and next when it was discovered that some Japanese on her manifest were missing. When at last she sailed, she was carrying seventy-three Japanese, including thirty from the Japanese Embassy in London who had been interned in a camp on the Isle of Man, and forty-three Thai citizens, Thailand having declared war on the Allies on 25 January 1942. En route to Lourenço Marques she bunkered and replenished

The *El Nil* in another view at Valletta on 21 January 1948. *Michael Cassar*

stores at St Vincent in the Cape Verde Islands on 9 August and at Walvis Bay, South West Africa (now Namibia), on 22 August.

The *Tatuta Maru* arrived in Shanghai on 3 August where she picked up more repatriates to add to those who had boarded her in Japan. She left for Saigon the next day, arriving there on 9 August. More exchange internees were collected, including the 104 from Thailand, before she sailed on 10 August to Singapore. At Singapore, two days later, she received the final additions to her exchange passengers, four Dutch civilians, and then set out alone across the Indian Ocean on 14 August.

The *Narkunda* was not officially part of the exchange mission until after she reached Durban. Prior to that, she sailed from the Clyde Estuary in routine troopship capacity as part of convoy WS21 bound for Sierra Leone. Five days were spent at Freetown where her participation in convoy WS21 ended and she probably received her exchange-mission markings while there. Departing Freetown on 15 August she reached Durban on 30 August and the following day proceeded to Lourenço Marques under safe-passage clearance carrying just 23 Japanese passengers, the only enemy repatriates she took aboard. However, she

Painted in her quite different mercy mission colours, NYK's *Tatuta Maru. Author's collection*

did also have a large quantity of Red Cross parcels destined to prisoners held in Japanese camps.

Meanwhile, the *Kamakura Maru* had begun her exchange voyage at Yokohama on 9 August. After a brief call at Kobe (11–12 August) she headed for Shanghai. Thus far, she had not carried any passengers for repatriation. Arriving empty on 16 August at Shanghai, she picked up her allotted 900 or so passengers and then headed for Singapore. At Singapore (23–24 August) she refuelled and replenished stores without berthing. As her complement had already been finalised, no additional exchange passengers were taken aboard. She then set off in the wake of the *Tatuta Maru*.

When the *Tatuta Maru* had set out from Yokohama she was carrying 454 British and Dominion internees. Among them were a number of high-profile VIPs – the British Ambassador Sir Robert Craigie, the Australian Chargé d'Affaires Keith Officer, the Belgian Ambassador, Ministers from Egypt, Greece and Czechoslovakia, and the Chargés d'Affaires of Norway and the Netherlands. With them were their wives and children and all diplomatic staff from Tokyo, Yokohama and Kobe. To these, 326 more passengers had been added at Shanghai, 144 at Saigon and four at Singapore. The composition of this eclectic gathering of 926 souls, all anxious to get home safely, makes interesting analysis. Split roughly

Seen in her peacetime colours, another superb view of P&O's *Narkunda*. *Allan Green*

one-third government officials and two-thirds bankers, lawyers, businessmen, teachers, missionaries and seamen, they comprised 729 of British and Dominion origin, sixty-nine Dutch, forty-seven Norwegian, thirty-one Belgian, twenty-three Polish, eleven Free French, seven Egyptian, six Greek, three Czech, and a Russian and an American – a truly international blend.

The *City of Paris*, the last of the six mission ships which had been under repair at Bombay since early June 1942, began her voyage to Lourenço Marques on 13 August, carrying 832 internees from India, the majority of whom were Japanese, along with a number of Thais. There had been a hitch when it was learned that Japan had not confirmed her safe-passage guarantee, but this was soon overcome. Three days later, the long and convoluted voyage of her fleetmate *City of Canterbury* commenced its next leg when she left Melbourne with another 834 exchange passengers, led by the Japanese Ambassador Kawai Tatsuo, carrying four boxes containing the ashes of killed Japanese submariners. A call at Fremantle was made on 21 August and from there she set off for East Africa on what was possibly the most challenging, solitary sea passage of the entire repatriation operation. At 4,900 nautical miles it was not quite the longest unbroken distance travelled by any of the mission ships, but on a relatively small vessel with so many occupants it could not have been a very comfortable voyage. To the credit of the officers and crew, when the Japanese passengers disembarked at Lourenço Marques a letter was passed to the ship's captain praising the courtesy, kindness and attention of the ship's company.

During her voyage to Lourenço Marques, totally oblivious to the attention she was receiving, the *Tatuta Maru* was observed and photographed by the submarine USS *Kingfisher*. *US Navy*

There was considerable overlap between the dates when the ships were present at the exchange port, both because of and potentially adding to the complications of what was an intricate transaction. Essentially, there were two elements to the exchange. First to arrive was the *Tatuta Maru* on 27 August, met the next day by the *City of Paris* and on 31 August by the *El Nil*. All the 948 occupants of the two British ships transferred to the *Tatuta Maru* along with a large quantity of Red Cross parcels. Of the *Tatuta Maru*'s passengers, approximately 400 transferred to the *El Nil*, including Ambassador Sir Robert Craigie and his team. Of the remainder, some boarded the *City of Paris* while others had to await the arrival of the *Narkunda* on 1 September and the *City of Canterbury* on 9 September. The *Tatuta Maru* remained in port until 2 September when she left on her return voyage, dropping off 571 Japanese and forty-two Thais at Singapore on 17 September and terminating her mission at Yokohama on 27 September 1942. She also took with her nearly 49,000 Red Cross parcels, the majority unloaded at Singapore.

The *Kamakura Maru* reached Lourenço Marques on 6 September, having passed the *Tatuta Maru* in mid-ocean. Of her occupants, 875 were relocated aboard the *Narkunda* – 115 on the *City of Canterbury* and the remainder on the other Ellerman Lines' ship. After she had loaded a large consignment of food parcels, the *Kamakura Maru* set off home on 11 September. She called first at Singapore where 454 passengers were disembarked and 14,770 parcels were discharged. The remaining 32,930 parcels were unloaded at Hong Kong on 4 October. She reached Yokohama on 8 October and two days later entered the naval base at Yokosuka for reconversion into an armed transport.

The *Kamakura Maru* at the time of the Anglo-Japanese exchange at Lourenço Marques.
Author's collection

The British ships remained at Lourenço Marques the longest. First to leave was the *El Nil* on 11 September. After a call at Cape Town she reached Liverpool on 9 October. Next was the *City of Paris* on 12 September after sixteen days in port. She made for Durban. The *Narkunda* followed on 13 September. On her homeward voyage she too called at Cape Town (17–18 September) and St Vincent (29 September–1 October). She entered Liverpool, completing her part of the mission, on 9 October.

Last to leave Lourenço Marques was the *City of Canterbury* on 16 September, also bound for Durban where she was reunited with the *City of Paris* and where both reverted to their wartime colours. But the saga did not end there. For the Indian, Australian and New Zealand internees who had been brought from Japan and the Far East and then taken to Durban, the subsequent phase of their journey home proved to be protracted and unsatisfactory, all of it without the protection of safe-passage guarantees.

The two Ellerman ships next sailed northwards on 19 September in Convoy CM 32, heading for Suez with a call at Aden, their repatriated passengers now caught up in routine war business. Still together, the pair left for Aden on 13 October where they parted their ways. The *City of Paris* headed straight to Bombay where she arrived on 27 October, while the *City of Canterbury* joined Convoy AP 4 to Basra and Bandar Abbās before joining Convoy PB 11 to Bombay on 10 November. She finally docked at Bombay on 16 November 1942. For some of the Indian repatriates, it had taken up to three and a half months to return home while the party of Australians and New Zealanders had been left to wait for space on passing ships heading south in order to get back to Sydney. Despite these hitches, a large and complex repatriation had been accomplished successfully. There were plans for a second Anglo-Japanese mercy mission, but for a variety of reasons it never occurred.

Mission 12: Berbera and Massawa, November 1942

At the time when a second relief mission to the former Italian colonies in East Africa was being discussed, it was calculated that there were still 11,718 persons waiting to be repatriated – 4,750 in Ethiopia and 6,300 in Eritrea plus 250 in Somalia, forty-eight at Berbera, 270 in Kenya and 100 in smaller dependencies. As this compared unfavourably with the estimated 9,600 capacity of the four ships, it was evident a third mission would be required, and this was taken into account in the planning of the second voyage.

The 270 persons in Kenya, all women and children, were to be taken to Tanga, Tanganyika (now Tanzania), and from there to Berbera aboard a British ship. The vessel that performed the transfer is not named in the records but is believed to have been British India Line's *Amra*, serving as Hospital Ship 41.

The limited berthing and port facilities at Mogadishu (now Hamar, Banaadir, Somalia), one of the planned destinations, necessitated the use of small craft for the transfer of passengers from shore to ship. This presented a major obstacle, even for passengers who were healthy, but for the sick or invalided awaiting repatriation at the port this method was considered impracticable. If no better means could be found to achieve a safe transfer, all the persons concerned would have to wait until the third mission took place, despite some cases of urgency.

As before, provisions were made for the ships to bunker and replenish en route. The *Arcola* and *Taigete* were to deliver fuel from Curaçao to Freetown on 24 July. Any residue in their tanks was to be topped up in a second call in the Netherlands East Indies and taken to Las Palmas (*Taigete*) and St Vincent in the Cape Verde Islands (*Arcola*). The Italians lodged a request for additional fuel supplies to be provided at Gibraltar, to be taken there by the tanker *Pagao*, which was then lying at nearby Algeciras. However, this was refused by the British, who insisted that the four liners should be fully bunkered before departing from Italy and that no late changes to arrangements would be countenanced.

On the first mission, the ships had also replenished at Port Elizabeth and, prior to their return, at Berbera. Supplies at the latter port and at Massawa (now Mitsawa, Eritrea) also needed to be augmented for refuelling on the second voyage, so the British authorities organised the movement of two tankers from Abadan, Persia (now Iran), to the exchange ports. The vessels selected for the task were the *British Chemist* of the British Tanker Company and the Norwegian-flag

Solfonn of Sigval Bergesen. As before, they required guarantees of non-molestation. This was sought from, and assurances to that effect confirmed by, the Italian authorities. Accordingly, they were painted in the colours previously adopted by the *British Genius* and *British Chancellor*. The *Solfonn* took diesel to Berbera for the two motorships, the *British Chemist* conveyed fuel oil for the turbine steamers to Massawa.

The *Duilio*, *Giulio Cesare*, *Saturnia* and *Vulcania* sailed together from Genoa on 21 October at the start of their second long repatriation voyage, eleven days later than had been originally planned. This was because the *Taigete* required repairs at Willemstad, which could not be carried out until approval for the work had been granted by the US Navy Department, in whose area of control Curaçao was located.

Signor Francesco Saverio Caroselli again headed the mission for the Italians. Also, as previously, the ships carried approved medical supplies, mail, books and parcels, mainly for those detainees who would have to attend the third repatriation mission. At Gibraltar, SBNOs boarded the ships with their armed parties and radio operators. They then followed the route specified for the first voyage, adhering to the same rules of conduct.

The *Saturnia* and *Vulcania* departed Gibraltar on 23 October 1942, called at Las Palmas (26–27 October) and Port Elizabeth (9–10 November) and arrived at

The *Duilio* displays her special colour scheme on her port side while berthed at Genoa. Among the repatriates collected by her and the *Giulio Cesare* were 415 who had travelled overland from Diredawa and Mandera. *Mario Cicogna*

The *Giulio Cesare* sailing on one of the East African mercy missions. *Mario Cicogna*

Berbera on 20 November 1942. The *Saturnia* and *Vulcania* then embarked a total of 5,285 repatriates.

The *Duilio* and *Giulio Cesare* departed Gibraltar on 24 October 1942, called at Las Palmas (27–29 October) and arrived at Port Elizabeth on 12 November 1942. From there, the *Duilio* departed on 14 November for Berbera (23–24 November) where she embarked 584 repatriates before continuing to Massawa, arriving there on 26 November 1942.

Meanwhile, the *Giulio Cesare* left Port Elizabeth on the same day bound for Massawa where she arrived on 24 November 1942. Between them, the *Duilio* and *Giulio Cesare* picked up an additional 3,652 persons making a total with those embarked at Berbera of 4,236. In combination with those of the *Saturnia* and *Vulcania*, the total number of repatriates on this mercy voyage was 9,521.

The ratios of these passengers was 40 per cent women, 36 per cent children up to fifteen years, 15 per cent infants below two and a half years and 8 per cent infirm men. The passengers included 253 priests and nuns; also among them were many who required hospital accommodation, which was provided on the *Duilio* and *Giulio Cesare*.

Having picked up the internees for return to Italy, the four liners set off on the return voyage, replenishing at Port Elizabeth and either St Vincent or Las Palmas. The *Saturnia* and *Vulcania* departed Berbera on 1 December 1942 and arrived

The *Saturnia* and *Vulcania* docked together during their stopover at Port Elizabeth. *Mario Cicogna*

at Port Elizabeth nine days later where it was discovered that eight Italian POW had stowed away, apparently with the connivance of crew members. The POW were arrested and ejected while an investigation was carried out by the SBNO en route to St Vincent to identify those who had been complicit. The two ships departed Port Elizabeth on 12 December, called at St Vincent (23–25 December), Gibraltar (31 December 1942–1 January 1943), Brindisi (6–7 January) and Venice (8–9 January), finally arriving at Trieste later the same day.

For their part, the *Duilio* and *Giulio Cesare* sailed from Massawa on 7 December 1942 and called at Port Elizabeth (18–20 December), Las Palmas (1–3 January 1943), Gibraltar (7–8 January), Brindisi (12–13 January) and Venice (14–15 January). They reached Trieste, the final destination, on 16 January 1943.

The Italian authorities had requested initially to have the four liners call at Naples on their return and from there have the *Saturnia* and *Vulcania* proceed to Trieste while the *Duilio* and *Giulio Cesare* would go to Genoa. Whereas the British Government was prepared to extend safe passage cover to forty-eight hours at each of the Italian ports of call, it declined to grant immunity at Naples because of planned or continuing military action. As a consequence, the disembarkation ports were amended with Brindisi replacing Naples. This was vital for the majority of the returning Italian internees because the homes of many were located in the country's southern regions.

Mission 13: Mersin, March 1943

Before the exchange of wounded and sick British and Italian servicemen was resumed at Smyrna, the *Gradisca* was engaged for a quite unusual, one-off repatriation mission, along with the British India liner *Talma* early in 1943. This mercy mission was organised by Great Britain and Italy, using Turkey as the intermediary, without any involvement of the ICRC. The fact that it was not in accordance with the stipulations of the Geneva Convention, in that none of the personnel exchanged were injured or suffering from long-term or incurable illness (all were able-bodied and healthy), may have had a bearing on this. Another peculiarity of this particular exercise was that the repatriates were intended to be exclusively naval personnel, and in fact the majority were.

The background to the exchange was a failed Italian naval operation at the time when British forces were rapidly advancing through the former Italian colonies in Somaliland and Eritrea and about to take the last of the key cities and ports. The remnants of the Italian fleet in the Red Sea were moored at Massawa, but as Asmara was about to be taken and the port would be the next objective for the British, the Commander of the Italian forces, Admiral Mario Bonnetti, ordered his destroyer squadron to sail to attack the British naval base at Port Sudan (now Bur Sudan) on 1 April 1941 in a last, desperate act of resistance. It was virtually a suicide mission, because the Italian ships were neither operationally ready nor adequately equipped for such an assault and stood little chance of surviving. There were six destroyers in total: *Cesare Battisti, Daniele Manin, Leone, Nazario Sauro, Pantera* and *Tigre*. Even as they were sailing, things started to go wrong when the *Leone* ran onto uncharted rocks off Massawa and, after she was abandoned, had to be sunk by gunfire from the *Pantera* and *Tigre*. Some records suggest that she was finished off by British aircraft.

British aerial reconnaissance soon discovered the remainder of the squadron and Swordfish aircraft from the British aircraft carrier HMS *Eagle* were sent to intercept it while naval vessels also gave chase. Firing their guns to the last, the *Daniele Manin* and *Nazario Sauro* were bombed and sunk, while the *Cesare Battisti* was ordered to withdraw and head for the Arabian coast where she was scuttled by her crew. The remaining two destroyers, *Pantera* and *Tigre*, constantly harassed by the British warplanes and unable to offer any serious resistance to the overwhelming firepower directed against them, were also ordered to break off and head across the Red Sea. They too were scuttled by their crews on the shores of Saudi Arabia.

Of course, the 550 or so Italian officers and sailors who landed from the abandoned ships could not be treated as prisoners of war because at that time Saudi Arabia had neutral status. By necessity, however, they were interned, but as internees they represented a significant encumbrance, both politically and from a welfare standpoint, on what was then a relatively undeveloped and backward desert kingdom. Consequently, the Saudi Government repeatedly appealed to the British Government for assistance in its endeavours to remove the unwanted Italians.

When, that June, the Turkish Government interceded, proposing a repatriation exchange as a possible solution to the quandary by swapping Royal Navy and

The hospital ship *Gradisca* completed four repatriation missions during 1943 beginning with the exchange of naval personnel at Mersin. *Mario Cicogna*

Royal Marines personnel held prisoner in Italy for the interned Italians, the Saudis immediately gave their support to this suggestion. Following discussions with the Italian authorities to gauge their reaction, Turkey next contacted the British Government to seek its views. Within days, on 11 October 1942, Great Britain signified its endorsement of the proposition and more detailed negotiations followed.

On 22 January 1943, the Italian Government indicated its acceptance of the finalised terms and arrangements for the exchange. The Turkish port of Mersin was selected as the location for the mercy mission and the date of the exchange was set for 20 March 1943. In the event, the numbers of persons exchanged was 788 from either side. According to contemporary reports, the numbers were swollen by having the naval personnel, who formed the core of the repatriates, supplemented by some additional British POW by one of the parties and by some Italian civilians and German sailors by the other. Whether or not these additional persons were in good health is not known.

The *Gradisca*, which was then in the Italian port of Bari, duly sailed for Mersin on 14 March 1943, while the *Talma* set out from Port Said on 18 March. As planned, they met at Mersin on 20 March, promptly completed the exchange and the *Gradisca* departed for Bari the very same day. The *Talma* left on her return voyage on 21 March 1943 and was back in Port Said three days later, bringing this unique repatriation exercise to a close.

Missions 14A and 14B, 15 and 16: Smyrna and Lisbon, April 1943; Smyrna, May and June 1943

For convenience, the three follow-on Anglo-Italian POW exchanges in the late spring and summer of 1943 are dealt with together. They were an extension to the first successful exchange, which had taken place in April 1942, and they were managed in accordance with the provisions that had been agreed for the original exercise, though there is no explanation as to why a year passed before the series was resumed. Another, fifth, exchange in September 1943 was not completed as planned because of the Italian capitulation and is dealt with separately.

There had been some concerns that Italy was not fully honouring the spirit of the agreement and that men who had been passed for repatriation by the Italian MMC had not been included in the first exchange, but this was not allowed to override the more pressing need to get as many of the sick and invalided soldiers as possible back to their homelands.

For the three Anglo-Italian missions in 1943, the numbers of transferred POW was much higher and, from necessity, more ships had to be recruited. For the April mission, the *Gradisca* met the British hospital ships *Tairea* and *Talamba* alone, while the *Newfoundland* completed the mission at Lisbon because of restrictions on the movement of ships through the western Mediterranean at that time, presumably because of intensification to the fighting in North Africa. The *Tairea* and *Talamba* also participated in the May and June exchanges, in which the *Gradisca* was joined for the Italian side by the former Tirrenia ships *Argentina* and *Città di Tunisi*. Each of these missions was relatively uncomplicated, the ships' movements on each as follows.

Beginning with the April exchange at Smyrna, the *Gradisca* set out from Bari to arrive at the Turkish port on 19 April 1943. Following the exchange, she departed

The *Newfoundland* departs Algiers on 31 March 1943 bound for Avonmouth to play her part in the repatriation at Lisbon in April 1943. *Lt C.H. Parnall, Crown Copyright*

the next day and returned to Bari. The *Tairea* and *Talamba* left Alexandria on 15 April 1943 to arrive at Smyrna four days later. The *Tairea* then sailed late on 20 April, the *Talamba* early on 21 April. Both ships reached Alexandria to disembark on 22 April 1943.

For the April exchange, at Lisbon, the *Newfoundland* departed Avonmouth on 11 April 1943 and arrived at Lisbon on 16 April. The *Newfoundland's* part of the mission received a lot of publicity. The Portuguese authorities were proud of their contribution to this and other acts of benevolence and readily publicised it. For example, a prominent feature, complete with pictures, appeared in the illustrated magazine *Século Illustrado*.

After the *Newfoundland* arrived at Portugal, she waited with her 409 Italian POW at the entrance of the River Tagus until she was informed of the arrival of two trains from Italy carrying 448 British POW. The trains terminated at the Alcântara Maritime station, within the port, and the *Newfoundland* then docked parallel to them at the adjacent quay. The Axis side used the occasion as an opportunity for pomp and propaganda. Both the German representative and the Italian Ambassador made speeches to the Italian POW during lunch in the building of the Portuguese Cod Fish Commission, following which they departed on the waiting trains. On the British side, a more dignified and discreet

Alongside at Lisbon, the *Newfoundland* in April 1943. Note that the crosses on either side of her funnel are not painted but attached in frames for night-time illumination. Her port-side boats are also swung out despite the fact she is docked at the quayside. *Século Illustrado*

approach to the affair was adopted and, apart from the more serious cases who were stretchered straight onto the *Newfoundland*, the remaining POW were taken for their lunch by bus to either of three locations – the English Club, the Seamen's Institute or the British Repatriation Office. Once embarked, the *Newfoundland* sailed on the evening of 18 April at 2200 hours, ending, in the words of *Diário de Lisboa*, 'one more admirable chapter of the humanitarian action of Portugal and the Red Cross in this war'. She arrived at Avonmouth on 23 April 1943, ending her participation in the repatriation process.

For the May exchange the *Gradisca*, *Argentina* and *Città di Tunisi* sailed together, again from Bari, arriving at Smyrna on 7 May 1943. Two days later they departed, returning to Bari. The *Tairea* and *Talamba* left Alexandria on 4 May 1943 and arrived at Smyrna on the same day as the Italian ships. They sailed on 10 May and were back in Alexandria two days later.

For the two Smyrna exchange missions of May and June 1943, the *Gradisca* was joined by the *Argentina*, seen in her unique colour scheme. *Mario Cicogna*

... and the *Città di Tunisi*, displaying her prominent 'PROTECTED' banner, both rare photographs. *Giorgio Spazzapan*

Finally, for the June exchange, the ships' movements followed a similar pattern. The voyage of the *Tairea* and *Talamba* from Alexandria commenced on 28 May 1943. By 1 June they were in port at Smyrna. As for the *Gradisca*, *Argentina* and *Città di Tunisi*, they again left Bari ensemble to arrive at Smyrna the next day. After a prompt transfer of passengers with little ceremony, they returned to Bari. The *Tairea* and *Talamba* sailed on the day after their arrival and were back at Alexandria by 5 June 1943.

The numbers of persons transferred in either direction during these missions, as recorded in various documents, are somewhat confusing. In some cases they may be referring to the as-planned numbers, in other cases the actual. It is feasible that some distortion may have arisen through the inclusion of certain civilians, though this cannot be corroborated. The only exchange for which there is reasonable certainty is that which involved the *Newfoundland*.

According to the report ICRC-1948, the repatriates in the Smyrna element of the April 1943 mission comprised 199 Italian POW and twelve protected personnel for 150 British POW and 200 protected personnel, while the figures for Lisbon were 409 Italians in exchange for 450 British. It is reported elsewhere that the April mission accounted for a total of 914 Italians exchanged for 1,916 British, a significant difference to the ICRC-1948 numbers, for which there is no explanation.

In May, at Smyrna, 2,411 Italian POW were exchanged for 400 British and, in June, 447 Italian POW and 2,229 protected personnel were transferred for

Representing the British side of the three Anglo-Italian repatriation exchanges at Smyrna in April, May and June 1943 were the *Talamba*, Hospital Ship 43, and... *Tom Rayner*

Hospital Ship 35, the *Tairea. Author's collection*

142 British POW and 293 protected personnel. Thus, using the ICRC-1948 figures, a total of 7,342 repatriates had been transported over the three missions. But that, too, does not equate to other figures, including those given for the *Gradisca* alone, the lead ship of the Italian contingent, which, according to *Le Navi Ospedale Italiane*, carried a total of 6,380 passengers, a combination of both nationalities, over her four outbound and return voyages in April 1942 and from April to June 1943. It is also claimed that in the course of the three 1943 missions a total of 9,014 were exchanged of whom 2,861 were British. None of these conflicting counts, which are simply presented here as recorded, can be reconciled.

Before the final, inconclusive Anglo-Italian repatriation took place, attention returned to the East African operation and the third and final voyage of that series.

Mission 17: Massawa, Mogadishu and Djibouti, June–July 1943

Discussions to arrange a third mercy voyage to collect Italian detainees in East Africa began in earnest in January 1943, immediately following the end of the second operation. Some preparatory work had been done to organise the fuelling logistics and this was accelerated because the setting of dates for the next voyage depended on having supplies in place.

Waiting in East Africa to be repatriated on the third voyage were mainly women, children and infirm men – 1,750 in Somalia and 5,150 in Eritrea – besides other categories of internees. The original intention of the British Government, in order to get the operation promptly concluded, was to have the ships dispatched no later than the middle of April 1943, but the sailings were delayed for technical reasons. By the time of the third voyage a number of complications had arisen, some in connection with the bunkering arrangements, others to do with the physical distribution of the remaining internees.

The *Arcola* and *Taigete* successfully completed the delivery of oil from Aruba to Las Palmas and St Vincent in good time, but there were difficulties in arranging replenishment facilities at the destination ports. The delay this caused only served to make matters worse for, with a later departure, the ships would arrive in the region of the Red Sea at the hottest time of year and it was considered undesirable for a ship loaded with repatriates to wait for any length of time in conditions of intense heat.

Wrestling with the problem, a number of options were tabled for consideration. One proposal was for all four ships to proceed first to Aden to refuel before heading to the embarkation ports. Another was for all four to go to Massawa to bunker prior to embarkation. While there, the *Saturnia* would then take aboard her passengers while the *Vulcania* would head to Mogadishu to pick up the repatriates at that port. From Massawa the *Saturnia* would continue to Djibouti before returning to Mogadishu to rendezvous with her sister ship. The main complication, however, apart from the refuelling, was the length of time it would take to transfer passengers at Mogadishu, bearing in mind that, for security reasons, the British wanted as far as possible to have the four ships kept in two pairs. It was calculated that it could take as long as ten days. The proposed solution was for one large and two smaller vessels, all three unnamed, to be placed on station to assist the embarkation. Another plan called for the *Saturnia* to go direct from Port Elizabeth to Djibouti and the *Vulcania* direct to Mogadishu and both to embark passengers before either ship bunkered for the return voyage.

Besides the organisational problems, it would seem that a number of anxieties had surfaced on the part of the British after the second mercy mission. Admiralty papers show that there was a fear, presumably with reasonable justification, that mines would be fitted in the liners' double bottoms, to be placed – how is not explained – in one of the Allied ports. There was also nervousness about stowaways after the incident at Port Elizabeth on the previous voyage. It was therefore stipulated that the ships were to remain incommunicado and subject to strict censorship throughout this final voyage, with no shore contact whatsoever permitted.

In the event, the arrangements ultimately settled on for the third voyage were a further deviation from the various schemes that had been assessed. The idea of taking bunkers at Aden was abandoned and instead the Swedish-flag tanker *Noravind* was chartered to take a consignment of fuel from Bandar Abbās to Massawa. The mercy ships' movements thus became as follows.

The *Saturnia* and *Vulcania* departed Trieste on 20 May 1943, called at Gibraltar (25–26 May), St Vincent (3 June) and Port Elizabeth (10–11 June), and arrived at Massawa on 21 June 1943. There the *Saturnia* embarked 2,298 repatriates and the *Vulcania* 2,239. These embarkations took five days and four days respectively to complete, the *Vulcania* moving on before the *Saturnia* had fully loaded. She continued to Djibouti where, by 6 July 1943, she collected fifty-five more passengers, after which she returned to Massawa.

Meanwhile the *Duilio* and *Giulio Cesare* had left Trieste two days behind the first pair on 22 May 1943, called at Gibraltar (28 May 1943), St Vincent (4 June 1943) and Port Elizabeth (17–18 June 1943) before arriving together at Mogadishu. In the absence of documentary evidence, it cannot be stated for certain how many internees were collected by the *Duilio* and *Giulio Cesare*, but they had more than adequate capacity and reportedly accommodated 2,218 internees. Given the total numbers returned from East Africa over the three missions, it is likely that the latter ships' complements were in fact considerably larger. Despite having a longer turnaround, it would seem that they boarded their passengers concurrently, a process expedited using the three vessels that had been made available to reduce the duration in port to the minimum.

The *Saturnia* departing from Trieste on 22 May 1943. To the left is the poop of the *Vulcania*. Further off is the *Duilio*. *Mario Cicogna*

As with the outbound voyages, some dates for the return passages are missing. Despite the desire to keep them together, the *Saturnia* departed Massawa ahead of the *Vulcania*. On her arrival at Port Elizabeth she was ordered to await the arrival of the *Vulcania* and during this time she boarded another 142 persons, presumably Italians, all from Southern Rhodesia.

After departing Port Elizabeth, the *Saturnia* and *Vulcania* called at St Vincent (2 August) to bunker and Gibraltar, finally arriving at Taranto on 21 August 1943. As for the *Duilio* and *Giulio Cesare*, they departed Mogadishu late that July, and called at Port Elizabeth, Las Palmas (13 August) and Gibraltar. Their voyage ended at Taranto on 31 August 1943. However, a further disembarkation may have taken place at Trieste, the subsequent destination of the four ships, two to meet their fate there, the other two to make their escape.

The arrivals of the ships in Italy occurred between two and twelve days prior to the cessation of hostilities with the Allies. Some of those who disembarked were fortunate enough to have landed in the south, in the area that had been liberated. The others, who may have travelled north, would suffer the months of fighting that followed before the Germans were finally driven out of Italy altogether.

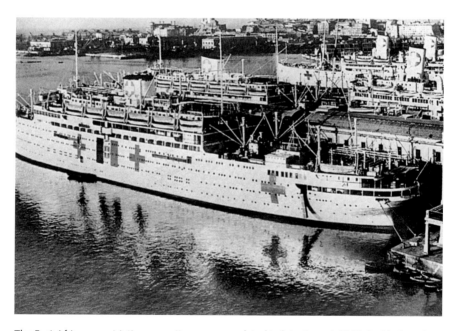

The East African repatriation operation was completed in late August 1943, just before the Italian Armistice. Here the Italian mercy fleet can be seen together at Genoa, the *Vulcania* nearest, next the *Saturnia*, *Giulio Cesare* and furthest to the right the *Duilio*. *Author's collection*

Mission 18: Lisbon and Algiers, September 1943

The fifth and, as it turned out, final Anglo-Italian repatriation had not been a certainty and was only first given consideration by the British in July 1943. When it did finally get underway, it was overtaken by events arising from the agreement of the Armistice of Cassibile with Italy, which, announced on the very day that the mission commenced, caused unforeseen consequences.

Under this repatriation, which was again subject to the rules of conduct agreed between Great Britain and Italy a year earlier, 115 British POW (the ICRC figure – other sources state 170) were to be exchanged for 555 Axis repatriates. These latter comprised 479 sick and disabled Italian POW, forty merchant seamen, twenty-one civilian internees of undisclosed nationality (probably Italian), seven women and children who had not been interned but who desired to return to Italy, and eight German civilians. Despite the mixed nature of this group, because the majority were POW the mission was subject to the provisions of the Geneva Convention, as had been the previous four.

The hospital ship *Atlantis* was selected for the operation, the arrangement being that she would take her exchange passengers to Lisbon, the eastern Mediterranean declared out of bounds. Simultaneously, the returning British POW would be taken to Portugal by train from Bergamo, Italy, east of Milan.

The *Atlantis*, then positioned on the River Clyde, off Greenock, sailed on 3 September for Avonmouth where, three days later, embarkation took place. She then sailed for Lisbon on 8 September, five days after the Armistice ending hostilities with Italy was proclaimed, but, although the war with Italy had been officially terminated, the country was still occupied by German troops whose fight continued, as became evident in the fierce resistance encountered by the advancing Allied armies. In these circumstances, all forms of communication, including the railway network, were appropriated by the Germans and it was impossible for the trains carrying the British POW to leave Italy. Although earlier permission had been granted for the trains to cross southern France, it was now refused. Of course, this also meant that the returning Italians would be prevented from reaching their home country, compelling them to remain in Portugal.

On 13 September, the *Atlantis* docked at Lisbon and deliberations ensued as to how to resolve a situation that none of the protocols had provided for. For all its goodwill, Portugal did not want to house and feed the Italian POW and internees. and the ICRC delegates were unhappy anyway about allowing them to disembark in the absence of the British POW on whose reciprocal return the mission was based. The report, ICRC-1948, suggests that despite this the POW did disembark but that the other repatriates, for whom there was no reciprocity, were not permitted to land. In fact, the complete reverse occurred, for it was the civilians among the repatriates who disembarked while the remainder, the

Hospital Ship 33, the *Atlantis*, at Naples in 1945. *Author's collection*

POW and the merchant seamen who Great Britain categorised as POW, were eventually landed at Algiers.

Thus, the *Atlantis* left Lisbon the day after her arrival, called at Gibraltar on 15 September and reached Algiers two days later. The repatriates were hastily disembarked and placed in detention while discreet shipping arrangements were organised, by which they were surreptitiously returned to the southern region of Italy, which by then was controlled by the Allies. Fully discharged, the *Atlantis* sailed from Algiers on 18 September bound for England, but on her arrival at Liverpool on 25 September, having come home empty, there was no fanfare or celebrations as had accompanied other returning mercy ships. By the following day she was back at Greenock, but at least at a later date she would participate in a more successful repatriation mission.

As for the 115 British POW, they were transferred to camps in Germany and Austria, despite concerted protests from the British Government. At the risk of compromising future exchanges, Germany gave as its explanation that it no longer recognised or accepted the rulings of the Italian MMC. Within two months, after Rommel quit North Africa leaving 250,000 German troops as prisoners, Germany was compelled to adopt a more conciliatory tone in its dealings on repatriation matters.

Mission 19: Mormugão, October 1943

Following the mission to Lourenço Marques, the *Gripsholm* had spent over nine months laid-up off Yonkers, New York, but she was reactivated in September 1943 to undertake the second civilian repatriation between the USA and Japan. Initiated as early as 29 July 1942 with a proposal and a preliminary list of persons for exchange, it was welcomed by the Japanese, although they countered with a tentative list of their own. From that point, matters were delayed by both the US War Department's reluctance to co-operate with the scheme and the inability of the American authorities to locate some of the listed persons. Planned sailing dates of 1 October and 1 December 1942 passed without progress. Frustrations, obstacles and protracted responses to communications caused repeated postponements continuing through the summer of 1943.

Although, optimistically, the Japanese had planned to use the *Conte Verde* and *Asama Maru* in another exchange at Lourenço Marques during October 1942. When the second mission finally went ahead they used the naval transport *Teia Maru*, the former French ocean liner *Aramis*. The selection of Lourenço Marques for the first exchange, approximately equidistant from the USA and Japan, had resulted in voyages of similar duration for the ships concerned, but for the second mission the port of Mormugão in neutral Portuguese Goa was chosen as the exchange location. This favoured the Japanese ship, but other than that no explanation can be found for the preference for the port on the Indian subcontinent. As the route would take the *Teia Maru* around Ceylon (now Sri Lanka), the British insisted, in granting safe passage, that it should pass at a greater distance out to sea, well away from the naval base at Colombo.

The *Gripsholm* was chartered again for the second US-Japan mercy exchange at Mormugao. *US Coast Guard*

The *Teia Maru* in her Japanese mercy-ship colours. Railway wagons were used to screen her repatriates and those from the *Gripsholm* from one another. *Author's collection*

With a longer voyage ahead of her, the *Gripsholm* was the first to sail, leaving New York on 2 September with a complement of 1,340 Japanese diplomats, bankers and businessmen, including 737 from Latin American countries. She also had 48,760 Red Cross parcels. Heading south, she called at Rio de Janeiro and Montevideo, collecting an additional eighty-nine and eighty-four repatriates respectively, before crossing the South Atlantic to Port Elizabeth. By now well established as a replenishment port for mercy missions, the *Gripsholm* took bunkers and loaded stores there. She then headed out across the Indian Ocean to arrive at Mormugão on 16 October 1943.

For her part, the *Teia Maru* began her mission at Yokohama on 14 September, calling briefly at Osaka before leaving there on 16 September bound for Shanghai (19–20 September). From Shanghai, she called at Hong Kong (22–23 September), San Fernando, Luzon in the Philippines (25–26 September), and Saigon (30 September). After two days anchored in the Malacca Strait, she entered Singapore (3–5 October). After taking on fuel, water and provisions, she set off for India sailing south-east around Sumatra, arriving in Mormugão on 15 October 1943. The ships docked adjacent to each other, their starboard sides to the quay, the *Gripsholm* ahead of the *Teia Maru*. It was not until three days later that the actual exchange took place, along with the transfer of the relief parcels.

Aboard the *Teia Maru* were around 1,512 British, US, Canadian and Latin American diplomats and internees, including many from the Santo Tomas,

Los Banos and Baguio camps in the Philippines, plus thirteen persons from neutral countries. There were also sixty Catholic priests and eighty nuns. Among the 975 repatriates collected in China were 660 missionaries and their families. The complements of both ships, in fact, changed during the course of their outward voyages through the birth of two Japanese babies on one ship and one American baby and the death of one missionary at Mormugão on the other.

Following the exchange, the ships remained in port for a few more days preparing for their return. The *Teia Maru* sailed on 21 October and the *Gripsholm* headed to sea a day later. The *Teia Maru*'s homeward voyage took her to Singapore (1–3 November) and Manila (7–9 November). She arrived back at Yokohama on 14 November 1943, disembarked her passengers and then resumed naval duties.

After eleven days at sea, the *Gripsholm* reached Port Elizabeth on 2 November. She sailed again on 4 November, called at Rio de Janeiro (15–16 November) and berthed at Jersey City on 1 December 1943.

There were plans to implement another, second, Anglo-Japanese exchange of non-combatants (initially due to take place at Mormugão in July 1943), as well as a third US-Japanese exchange. Ultimately, neither took place. There were simply too many complications and obstacles, in the former case primarily because of opposing views on the status of merchant seamen. Because the Japanese insisted

The *Teia Maru* alongside at Mormugao in October 1943. *L.L. von Münching collection*

on dealing with its two main adversaries separately, they would not conclude another American mission until a second British one had been dealt with first. The US repeatedly urged the British to expedite negotiations with the Japanese but they fell at every hurdle. Realistically, though, with the war rapidly closing in on the Japanese homeland, the China Sea had become a deadly place to navigate as Allied submarines were able to pick off enemy ships virtually at will. Routes over which civilians could be safely transported were becoming harder to find.

Missions 20A, 20B and 20C: Gothenburg, Barcelona and Oran, October–November 1943

With Italy out of the war, all efforts were concentrated on maintaining exchanges with Germany as well as, if possible, Japan. Arising from the failure of the October 1941 mission, there had not so far been an Anglo-German repatriation. In September 1943, the USA and Germany had reached an agreement for the mutual exchange of seriously sick and injured POW along with protected personnel over and above those required to provide medical care for prison camp inmates. For the purposes of the agreement, the personnel for retention were calculated on the basis of two doctors, one dentist, one chaplain and six other enlisted medical ranks for each 1,000 POW. Those in excess of that number could be repatriated, a situation that made for some hard choices among those concerned – who could go and who had to stay?

By the time the first repatriation under the agreement took place in October 1943, Britain had been absorbed into the pact, having itself proposed a comprehensive process of regular exchange of civilian internees and POW with Germany on 9 August 1943. This marked the start of greater collaboration in these affairs by Great Britain and the USA that continued through to the end of the war.

Britain had already undertaken an extremely intricate exchange with the Japanese in September 1942. Along with the USA, it was now about to embark upon an equally complex repatriation mission with the Germans. The mission consisted of three related phases, the physical exchanges due to take place at different ports – Gothenburg, Barcelona and Oran in Algeria. This called for an extraordinary amount of organisation and planning involving several Red Cross organisations and various military, harbour and transport authorities. No fewer than thirteen ships would participate, nine of them ocean liners, plus a small cruise ship, a coastal steamer and two train ferries. A final transfer, after the official exchange had finished, would engage the services of another former liner.

There are discrepancies in the numbers quoted by different sources for the numbers repatriated in this mission, which are now impossible to reconcile so long after the event. However, ICRC-1948 states that a total of 5,765 German

Here the *Drottningholm* is under charter to Great Britain for the first repatriation exchange arranged at Gothenburg. *Crown Copyright*

nationals (1,146 sick and injured POW, 4,341 protected and medical personnel, 176 merchant seamen and 102 civilian internees) were exchanged for 5,195 Allied persons (3,112 sick and disabled POW, 1,826 protected and medical personnel, 152 merchant seamen and 105 civilian internees).

At Gothenburg, three ships – two British and one Swedish – arrived from Britain and America with 832 German nationals. Simultaneously, hospital trains collected 4,159 Allied POW, internees and others who qualified for repatriation from Stalags and prison camps across Germany, Holland and France, among them the men who had been denied repatriation in the cancelled Newhaven–Dieppe exchange, and began ferrying them to either Swinemünde or Sassnitz on Germany's Baltic coast. Many of the civilians were from the Vittel camp near Épinal in the Vosges, south of Nancy. From Swinemünde, prisoners and detainees boarded either of two small ships: the one-time Norwegian-flag cruise ship *Meteor* or the Baltic steamer *Rügen*, both registered hospital ships. They were taken direct to Gothenburg. From Sassnitz, either of two train ferries, the *Deutschland* or *Drottning Victoria*, conveyed others to Trelleborg in southern Sweden, each returning empty to complete at least two crossings. The Swedes had laid on hospital trains of their own and these next took the repatriates landed at Trelleborg overland to Gothenburg.

Meanwhile, four ships, two each for Germany and the Allies, met in Barcelona for their part of the exchange. Barcelona had been selected in place of Smyrna in order to provide for subsequent movements of the German ships within

The movement of British POW from camps in Germany across the Baltic to Sweden, via Sassnitz and Trelleborg, required the services of two train ferries, the *Drottning Victoria*, shown here, and the *Deutschland*. *Author's collection*

stipulated timeframes. The British ships had aboard them 1,057 German POW, protected personnel and internees embarked at Port Said, while their German counterparts had collected 1,036 Allied and Commonwealth POW and protected personnel – Australians, New Zealanders, Indians and Palestinians – from Marseilles, the majority of whom had been taken there by train from Lamsdorf (now Łambinowice) concentration camp in Silesia, a 500-mile journey from Poland across Czechoslovakia and southern Germany.

Finally, four German-controlled ships, including both of those used in the Barcelona part of the exchange, proceeded from Marseilles to Oran in Algeria, to pick up 3,876 Germans, 342 of whom were POW who had been captured and held in Tunisia, the remainder protected personnel.

Of the main mission ships at Gothenburg, the *Drottningholm*, which had crossed from New York, was the first to dock. US State Department papers suggest that 234 incapacitated POW and 1,732 protected personnel were shipped to Europe aboard her, but these figures cannot be correlated with the ICRC numbers and they may include elements of personnel exchanged at the other ports. Meanwhile, the *Atlantis* sailed outbound from Greenock on 14 October 1943 carrying 788 sick and wounded German POW plus a quantity of civilian internees. The *Empress of Russia* left Liverpool the same day. Together they sailed around Scotland, transiting the Pentland Firth.

All three ships had to clear British Contraband Control at Tōrshavn in the Faroe Islands and German Contraband Control at an anchorage off Kristiansand, Norway. From there, German quartermasters steered the ships to Strömstad before they were led through a safe channel into Gothenburg by Swedish minesweepers. First of the latter pair to arrive was the *Empress of Russia* on 19 October followed two days later by the *Atlantis*. The trains from Trelleborg arrived at Gothenburg early on 18 October and even before dawn many of the repatriates had been

The third British mercy ship at Gothenburg in October 1943 was the *Empress of Russia*. British Pathé

With the train ferries were two hospital ships operating between Swinemünde and Gothenburg. This is the *Rügen*. WZ-Bilddienst

transferred to the waiting *Drottningholm*. Around midday, the *Meteor* and *Rügen* docked at the quayside. Transfers to the *Empress of Russia* began immediately after her arrival in the afternoon of the following day, and later to the *Atlantis* after she docked astern of the *Meteor*. By then the *Drottningholm* had vacated her berth and made for the island of Vinga, 10 miles to the west, to make compass adjustments for the return to Great Britain.

It was said that the Allied ships at Gothenburg were required to wait for a signal from Oran signifying that the phase of the mission conducted there had been completed satisfactorily before they were permitted to leave for England. However, the dates of the physical transfers and the ships' movements would not appear to support this supposition. Both the *Empress of Russia* and the *Drottningholm*, waiting off Vinga, sailed on 21 October, followed a day later by the *Atlantis*. The *Empress of Russia*'s first home call was at Methil, in the Firth of Forth (25–26 October), and she may also have docked briefly at Leith before she proceeded around Scotland to reach Glasgow on 29 October. The *Atlantis* returned direct to Liverpool with the *Drottningholm*, both arriving there on 26 October 1943. The complement of returning British servicemen aboard the Atlantis – the only exact figure known – was 790.

In the meantime, the *Cuba* and *Tairea* had set off for Barcelona, leaving Port Said together on 19 October. They arrived at Barcelona six days later and berthed at one end of the vast landing stage. Docked at the opposite end, separated from them by three rows of warehouses, were the hospital ship *Aquileia* with the former liner *Djenné*, both now in German hands. Those prisoners who were fit enough were required to walk the length of the wharf as they transferred between the ships.

Conducting the affairs at Barcelona were General Moscardó for the Spanish authorities, the British Ambassador Sir Samuel Hoare and his German

In preparation for the second part of the big Allied-German exchange of late 1943, the *Cuba* sailed from Port Said to Alexandria on 19 October. *Raymond Chevalier courtesy of Jean-Yves Brouard*

The four mercy ships at Barcelona on 27 October 1943, the *Tairea* and *Cuba* on the left and the *Aquileia* and *Djenné* on the right. Note the queue of POW repatriates filing along the quayside. *La Vanguardia courtesy of Jean-Yves Brouard*

On the quayside at Barcelona, an incongruous mix of Anzac troops queuing for transfer and uniformed German officials in the foreground, including the imposing German Ambassador to Spain, Dr Hans-Heinrich Dieckhoff. In the background, the swastika markings on the *Djenné* can be clearly seen. *Klaus Günther von Martinez collection*

The hospital ship *Aquileia*. Like the *Tairea* she conveyed wounded and sick POW, while the *Djenné* and *Cuba* transported Protected Personnel and other repatriates. *Mario Cicogna*

The *Djenné* is greeted by nurses at Marseilles as she arrives with repatriated German POW. *Klaus Günther von Martinez collection*

counterpart, Dr Hans-Heinrich Dieckhoff, along with the ICRC delegate Dr Abenz. By 27 October the exchange was complete and all four ships had departed. The *Cuba* and *Tairea* returned to Alexandria in consort, arriving there on 3 November. The following day the *Cuba* left for Port Said, reaching the Suez Canal port on 5 November. The *Tairea* required voyage repairs lasting until 19 November before she too sailed to Port Said.

The *Aquileia* and *Djenné* left Barcelona on 27 October with Marseilles as their first port of call to disembark the prisoners collected at Barcelona. Joined there by the hospital ships *Gradisca*, which had relocated from Patras, Greece, and *Sinaia*, the quartet then made the crossing to Oran, all four ships needed in order to accommodate the almost 4,000 German repatriates waiting there.

Along with the *Djenné*, *Gradisca* and *Aquileia*, the hospital ship *Sinaia* took part in the Oran element of the big 1943 Allied-German exchange, taking German POW to Marseilles. The photograph shows the *Sinaia* earlier in the war, at Beirut in 1941, while repatriating French troops to Marseilles. *Jean-Yves Brouard collection*

Soldiers who had lost limbs disembark from the *Aquileia* at Marseilles after their arrival from Oran. *Jean-Yves Brouard collection*

The *Cuba* returned to Alexandria following the Barcelona exchange. The photograph shows her in the Egyptian port on 3 November 1943. *G.R. Bull courtesy of Jean-Yves Brouard*

On their arrival at Suez aboard the *Tairea*, repatriated Australian and New Zealand POW were transferred to the hospital ship *Oranje* for the final, long voyage to their home countries. *L.L. von Münching*

The Axis fleet's return to Marseilles brought the entire mission to an end, but, in connection with an associated supplementary voyage, it was well into that December before the last of the POW reached home. After calling at Port Said, the *Tairea* immediately sailed through the Canal on 21 November where the hospital ship *Oranje* was waiting for her at Suez. The *Oranje* had sailed there especially from Durban, bunkering at Aden en route for what was to be a long voyage. The Anzac prisoners exchanged at Barcelona were transferred to the *Oranje*, which took them initially to Melbourne, arriving there on 10 December 1943, almost two months after the official exchange had ended, before continuing to Wellington.

Despite its quite involved composition, this repatriation, one of the largest of the war, had gone well in all its phases. It was a positive outcome that bode well for subsequent mercy missions over the next eighteen months.

Missions 21, 22 and 23: Lisbon, March 1944; Barcelona, May 1944; Lisbon, July 1944

Between March and July 1944, three smaller repatriation missions took place, two at Lisbon and one at Barcelona. By this time, as the large October 1943 mission had demonstrated, the rules relating to the different categories of repatriates were becoming blurred and the principle that POW and civilian internees should be processed separately was progressively disregarded. The pressing need to evacuate as many as possible from the deteriorating and increasingly lethal situation in Germany and its occupied territories overrode other considerations, and it was accepted by the ICRC too that joint ventures had become the order of the day. In all of the next three missions, both POW and civilian internees were exchanged together.

In June 1942, at the end of the *Drottningholm*'s second exchange at Lisbon, it had been concluded by the US authorities that there were few, if any, of its citizens still incarcerated in Europe requiring more recovery expeditions. While this may not have been entirely the case, there were, however, a great many Latin-American internees held in Germany and, as the USA had become the de facto repository for interned enemy aliens for the American Republics, a large percentage brought from South and Central America, there was scope for a transfer of these persons. This took place in early 1944 at Lisbon. Again the *Gripsholm* was the ship used.

In the correspondence between German Government departments, a letter dated 19 February 1944 notes that, arising from a mutual alignment of objectives, the *Gripsholm* was expected to leave New York on 15 February and arrive at Lisbon on 24 February. She would be bringing 1,240 repatriates, comprising 1,108 German civilians who had been in Latin American countries, 118 seriously wounded POW

The Latein-Amerikanischer Verein letter of 19 February 1944 referring to the *Gripsholm's* exchange voyage from New York. *German American Internee Coalition*

from the USA and fourteen naval POW from Canada. These repatriates were to be taken back to Germany by train and it was anticipated that they would arrive in Saarbrücken, just across the border from France, on 29 February.

Other records have dates that are at variance with those in the official German letter, implying that, for some unknown reason, the *Gripsholm's* departure was delayed. They give the *Gripsholm's* arrival at Lisbon as 4 March 1944 and her re-entry into Jersey City at the end of the return voyage on 15 March. The precise number of detainees and prisoners who returned with the *Gripsholm* is not known, but, given that equivalence was generally insisted upon for civilian exchanges, it would have been comparable to the complement brought across from North America.

For the next exchange, which in fact took place in two parts, Barcelona was again selected as the main location. The first component, in February 1944, was performed at Irún, north Spain, near the Spanish–French border, and witnessed the release of just thirty-six seriously wounded British and American servicemen. How they got home is not explained, but US State Department papers for 1944 confirm both the exchange and the numbers. Three months later, on 17–18 May, the main element of the exchange transpired at Barcelona. Two ships were involved – the *Gripsholm* on her fourth mission for the Allies and the *Gradisca* on her seventh mission for Axis countries.

The *Gradisca*, which had been lying at Venice, sailed to Marseilles on 4 May 1944 where she embarked 1,043 (Spanish reports say 1,021) American and British POW and sixty-five internees. Among those categorised as POW were a group of merchant seamen. This diverse party of prisoners had reached Marseilles aboard four trains, one from the German holding camp at Annaburg, south of Potsdam, another from Berlin, which, on a circuitous route, had collected repatriates from the Posen (now Poznán) and Lamsdorf Stalags as well as hospital

The *Gradisca* returned to Barcelona for another exchange in May 1944. *WZ-Bilddienst*

cases from Neustettin (now Szczecinek). Following one after the other, about an hour apart along the same track, they took different routes to Marseilles after entering French territory for security reasons. From Marseilles the *Gradisca* proceeded direct to Barcelona.

Still under charter to the United States, the *Gripsholm* sailed from New York to Algiers on 2 May 1944 where 857 (Spanish reports say 833) German wounded and members of medical corps, some in the custody of Free French forces, were waiting to be handed over. From Algiers, the *Gripsholm* made for Barcelona, docking there around midnight on 17 May, one hour ahead of the *Gradisca*, which had left Marseilles ten hours earlier.

Every effort was made to keep the respective prisoner groups apart to avoid antagonism and, though the ships were berthed alongside the same quay, the adjacent warehouses were used to provide separate transfer routes between them. On completion of the exchange, the *Gradisca* returned to Marseilles where her German passengers boarded trains for conveyance back to their homeland. Subsequently, the *Gradisca* was repositioned at Porto d'Ascoli on the Adriatic coast, south of Ancona, where she docked on 12 June 1944. It was the end of her last mission as a mercy ship.

The *Gradisca* was met at Barcelona by the *Gripsholm* serving the interests of Allied governments, principally the United States and Great Britain. The repatriates exchanged were a mix of POW, protected personnel and internees. *US Navy*

The *Gripsholm* sailed for the UK via Algiers (21 May), making her disembarkation call at Belfast (27–28 May) for around 1,000 POW before continuing to New York with the remaining sixty-five, some of whom may have been among the thirty-six transferred in February. Belfast had been appointed as the British terminus because, due to the intense activity in the run-up to D-Day, the *Gripsholm* was not permitted to enter a port on the UK mainland. This necessitated the transfer of the returning POW to a 'west of England port', probably Liverpool, by unnamed Irish Sea ferries. The majority of these vessels were by then in service as naval auxiliaries. The only possible candidates, therefore, were the 2,017grt *Louth*, later renamed *Ulster Duke*, or the 1,913grt *Longford*.

Barely a month after the *Gripsholm* had returned to New York, her fleetmate *Drottningholm* set off for Lisbon on 12 July 1944 on another repatriation mission, the third of this series. Little in the form of archived documents seems to have survived concerning this exchange. The repatriates were German and Allied POW with some internees among them, but their numbers have not been discovered. By the time of her arrival at Lisbon in early August after what was, if the recorded dates are correct, an unusually long Atlantic crossing (although she may have called at Liverpool en route) trains from the camp at Vittel, 20 miles west

Two repatriated US airmen gaze out over Liverpool docks from one of the *Gripsholm*'s gangplanks. The date was 28 May 1944, before the *Gripsholm* continued to New York. *Author's collection*

of Épinal, began to arrive in the Portuguese capital. The exchange completed, the *Drottningholm* left Lisbon on 4 August bound for Liverpool. For some reason she was instructed to follow a course around the west coast of Ireland to approach Liverpool from a northerly direction via the North Channel, to arrive there on 9 August 1944. Now chartered to the British Government, the *Drottningholm* remained at Liverpool from where she participated in the next Gothenburg mission in September 1944.

Mission 24: Lisbon, August 1944

Diplomatic repatriations had taken place between Germany and both Brazil and Chile, although details of these exercises, mentioned in documents at The National Archives, Kew, cannot be found. It is feasible that they were incorporated into the missions arranged by the USA, such as that at Lisbon in March 1944 (Mission 21), as many detainees from those countries had been deported to America, as explained earlier.

The situation with regard to Argentina was quite different. Argentina had enjoyed good relationships with Germany over a long period and was reluctant to join the Allied cause. There was also resentment of unjustifiable claims that it was a hotbed of Nazi sympathisers. Equally, it objected to the coercive political pressure applied on it by the American Government to get it to change its stance. Ultimately, though, Argentina *did* break off diplomatic relations with both Germany and Italy on 26 January 1944. The very next day, Argentina and Germany entered into discussions with regard to the exchange of diplomats and the return of Argentine citizens from Germany and other countries that had joined the Axis. But the negotiations were beset by issues and the mission itself had an unsatisfactory conclusion.

Communications between Great Britain and the United States, during the time when these bipartite talks were ensuing, reveal significant reservations that could have prejudiced the granting by them of safe conduct for the mission. There was unease about the possible smuggling of contraband war materials, principally industrial diamonds, platinum and mica but also pharmaceuticals and tinned foodstuffs, from Argentina. There was also concern that a well-intentioned mercy mission might inadvertently provide the means of return to Germany of escapees from the interned crew of the German pocket battleship *Admiral Graf Spee*, which had been scuttled in the River Plate on 17 December 1939. This disquiet was amplified when it became known that the Argentine Foreign Office was proposing to conduct the repatriation exchange in a French port. The subsequent selection of Lisbon for the mission helped allay some of these apprehensions.

Another complication was Germany's insistence on having other categories of persons besides diplomatic staff and private citizens embraced by the operation, among them professors, schoolmasters, crews of merchant ships and representatives of travel organisations, all of which raised further objections from Britain and America.

For its part, the British Government wanted the ships engaged for the mission to be cleared by Contraband Control at Trinidad because they would be passing within the maritime jurisdiction of the Allies en route to Lisbon. It called for a thorough search of the vessels, along with the persons they would be carrying and their baggage, to be carried out in the presence of a Swiss Government representative, Mr Nikolas J. S. Gonzenbach.

When the identities of the ships to be utilised became known, Britain's insistence on strict security controls was relaxed somewhat, although it still persisted with its requirement for a measure of contraband clearance. Of the two ships, the *Cabo de Buena Esperanza*, presumably chartered from the Ybarra Compania for the purpose, had neutral status and as such qualified for a warrant, a trust device that permitted vessels to proceed with minimal inspection. The other ship, the *Rio Jáchal* – a former French ship seized by Argentina on 28 July 1943 after three years of lay-up at Buenos Aires and allocated to the state shipping company – did not carry a warrant. However, Britain offered to implement the NaviCert system in respect of the *Rio Jáchal*. It also proposed that both ships could be inspected at Buenos Aires prior to departure by British Embassy officials or examiners flown out especially from the UK.

These deliberations inevitably introduced delays, and a planned departure of 10 March 1944 slipped to early May and then to 4 June. Even then, complications and obstacles remained to be resolved. Germany had countered Britain's position by stating that it would not check Argentine baggage if the personal luggage of its citizens was not scrutinised either. No matter how sensitive it was to Argentina's situation, though, Britain remained adamant about its security stipulations. America, on the other hand, worried about keeping Argentina on side and more bothered about possible espionage and fifth-columnist activity within an allied American republic, adopted a more pragmatic attitude, declaring that the repatriation was essential and that having it take place overrode all other considerations.

Even as it seemed that all impediments had been resolved, another potential problem surfaced. The *Rio Jáchal* had been seized from the French and it was now feared that, on arrival at Lisbon, the French Committee of National Liberation (essentially the Free French Government in exile) would claim the ship through the Portuguese courts. However, Portugal recognised the Vichy Government and it was felt that the Vichy French would not press for the ship unless instigated

A significant mercy mission in which neither the USA nor Great Britain participated was an exchange arranged between Germany and Argentina, which did not result exactly as intended. The appropriated former French liner *Campana*, renamed *Rio Jáchal* and seen here in her 'DIPLOMATICOS' colour scheme, took German diplomats and internees to Lisbon in consort with the Spanish liner *Cabo de Buena Esperanza*. Although the mission agreement specified the number of diplomats to be exchanged, in the event none were returned to Argentina. *Histarmar courtesy of Archivo General de la Nacion – Dep. Fotografia BS AS Argentina*

to do so by Germany. But because Germany had already granted safe-conduct guarantees for the *Rio Jáchal* this was considered unlikely.

At last the ships sailed, carrying between them 293 Germans, three Chileans, three members of the Bulgarian legation to Argentina, one Peruvian passenger and 210 persons of other nationalities. Whereas the *Rio Jáchal* would sail direct to Trinidad, the *Cabo de Buena Esperanza* would call at ports en route. She left Buenos Aires on 6 July, called at Montevideo (8 July), Guanabara Bay in Rio de Janeiro (11–13 July), Puerto Cabello in Venezuela (25 July) and Curaçao (26 July) before returning eastwards to arrive at Trinidad on 28 July 1944. The *Rio Jáchal*, which sailed from Buenos Aires on 12 July, reached Trinidad a day ahead of the *Cabo de Buena Esperanza*. After the mandatory security checks, the two ships headed via the Azores to Lisbon where they arrived on 14 August, only for their ship's companies to find themselves confronting a fresh quandary.

Owing to the advancing liberation of France, the Germans had been unable to get the Argentine diplomats (gathered from Germany as well as Italy, France, Bulgaria, Rumania, Hungary and Denmark) across the border into Spain and from there to Portugal. In an attempt to redeem the situation, Germany suggested that the *Rio Jáchal* should continue to Gothenburg with her German repatriates while the *Cabo de Buena Esperanza* remained behind in Lisbon with her passengers until the exchange had been satisfactorily finalised in Sweden. This would have entailed considerable additional route planning and safe-passage arrangements at a time of intensified military activity following the invasion of Normandy. Britain counter-proposed that the Argentine diplomats who were unable to reach Lisbon, approximately 120 in total, could instead be included in the next Allied exchange scheduled to take place at Gothenburg in early September, provided that they did not displace any American or British POW or civilians who were being released. From Gothenburg they could be taken aboard the *Gripsholm* to New York for collection by an Argentine vessel.

As it turned out, neither of these options was adopted. The *Rio Jáchal* instead boarded 267 non-diplomatic Argentine subjects, mostly women and children who had been left destitute in Vigo, Spain, plus one Chilean and two Bolivian diplomats. She left Lisbon on her return passage on 7 September, called again at Trinidad and arrived at Buenos Aires on 6 October 1944 to a crowded welcome of local citizens, Government officials and journalists and photographers from Argentine and Brazilian newspapers. The *Cabo de Buena Esperanza* sailed from Lisbon a few days after the *Rio Jáchal*. In so doing she may have resumed her intermittent line service between Spain and Argentina, as there was no mention of repatriates when she docked at Buenos Aires on 17 October 1944.

As for the diplomats who had been denied repatriation, they were taken to Gothenburg where they remained until 14 March 1945. They then joined the *Drottningholm* on her last, long mercy mission to Turkey. After a call at Liverpool, they disembarked at Lisbon on 28 March 1945 but were compelled to endure yet another month of waiting there. When finally, on 7 May 1945, they embarked on the *Cabo de Hornos*, the sister ship of the *Cabo de Buena Esperanza*, they were able to return to Argentina without fear of attack and without the need for safe-passage guarantees as the war with Germany had ended. Their long ordeal ended on 17 June 1945 when at last they stepped ashore in Buenos Aires.

The *Cabo de Hornos*, sister ship of the *Cabo de Buenos Esperanza*, which finally conveyed the Argentine diplomats to Buenos Aires. *Histarmar courtesy of Archivo General de la Nacion – Dep. Fotografia BS AS Argentina*

Mission 25: Gothenburg, September 1944

The next big exchange again took place at Gothenburg, requiring three large passenger ships plus the smaller steamers and train ferries that had been allocated previously.

The tide of the war had turned irreversibly against Germany, and with far greater numbers of prisoners in Allied custody there was increased willingness to support the repatriation initiatives. Delegates of the International Red Cross in Germany had become more active, too, able to apply more pressure for concessions and able to gain access to prisoners, hitherto denied, as some among the Nazi hierarchy sensed the need to be seen as more conciliatory and compassionate.

With the exchange scheduled for 8–9 September, the *Arundel Castle*, *Drottningholm* and *Gripsholm* made their way to the Swedish port, between them carrying 2,136 repatriates, comprising 1,553 sick and wounded German POW, 583 civilian repatriates, thirty-four German Red Cross nursing sisters and eighty-three merchant seamen. (These figures, from ICRC-1948, do not add up, an error, perhaps, in the writing of the report. In fact, they make a total of 2,263.) To embark her share, the *Arundel Castle* sailed from Greenock to Liverpool on 28 August 1944 and, after five days in port, left for Gothenburg on 2 September along with the *Drottningholm*.

Among the ships engaged for the second big Gothenburg exchange was the Union-Castle liner *Arundel Castle*. *Author's collection*

The Swedish America Line ships *Drottningholm* and *Gripsholm* were again chartered to assist the *Arundel Castle*. Here the *Gripsholm* is assisted by tugs at her peacetime homeport. *Sjöfartsmuseet Akvariet*

The *Drottningholm* had arrived back in Liverpool on 30 August, the day after the *Arundel Castle*'s arrival, after making a run to North Africa as the first part of her mission to pick up German POW from Bône (now Annaba), Algeria.

After their arrival in Gothenburg on 8 September, the *Arundel Castle* and *Drottningholm* were later joined by the *Gripsholm*, which again had crossed the Atlantic, calling at Londonderry and Liverpool en route. Her arrival at Gothenburg was delayed through an incident at Kristiansand when German officials boarded the ship and ordered her into port. It was only when the ship's master, Captain Harry Gunnar Nordensen, protested vehemently, asserting his ship's rights as a safe-conduct cartel ship, that he was permitted to proceed without further interference.

The arrangements for the transfer of returning Allied POW and civilian internees from Germany were identical to those adopted for the October 1943 exchange (Mission 20), utilising the *Meteor* and *Rügen* between Swinemünde and Gothenburg and the train ferries *Drottning Victoria* and *Deutschland* between Sassnitz and Trelleborg, with a rail connection to Gothenburg. All told, they conveyed a total of 2,654 Allied personnel. The majority, some 1,988, were sick and wounded POW. The numbers of civilian repatriates and merchant seamen corresponded exactly to those returned by the Allies.

As in the previous Gothenburg mission, among the vessels used for the transfer of exchanged POW across the Baltic between Germany and Sweden was the former cruise ship *Meteor* serving as a German hospital ship. *WZ-Bilddienst*

While the German repatriates made their way back to Germany via the ferries and small steamers, the three big ships returned to Liverpool. All three sailed on 10 September and were back in the Mersey by 16 September, another gala occasion with welcoming dignitaries and a sizeable presence of local folk, as well as newsreel cameramen and members of the local and national press.

After she had completed her disembarkation, the *Gripsholm* set off for New York while the *Arundel Castle* returned to Greenock on 17 September. The *Drottningholm* remained in Liverpool until 16 October when she sailed back to her Swedish homeport. She cleared Kristiansand around 23 October 1944 and docked at Gothenburg four days later. After spending the winter months there, she was reactivated the following March, chartered by the German Government for her final mercy mission.

Mission 26: Marseilles, January 1945

The Allied advance through Italy and, after Operation *Dragoon*, southern France, along with the almost complete eradication of an enemy threat to shipping in the Mediterranean, again favoured the use of ports in that region for repatriation.

Strictly speaking, Marseilles, which was liberated on 27 August 1944, was not an exchange port for the January 1945 mission, only a delivery and collection port. A further development arising from the progress of the war against Germany was its increasing inability to access ports in Portugal, Spain, Italy or southern France, so that in some instances landlocked exchanges became necessary, sponsored by the Swiss Government. Thus, the January 1945 exchange took place physically at Kreuzlingen, just across the border from Konstanz on the Bodensee, which was still accessible by rail from Germany. This required the ferrying of repatriates from the United States and Great Britain to Marseilles and their entrainment into Switzerland via Geneva. Unusually, the January 1945 exchange was negotiated almost exclusively by the Swiss Government acting as the Protecting Power for both parties.

Three Allied ships were deployed for the mission. The *Gripsholm*, with the hospital ship *Letitia*, sailed from Jersey City carrying 989 and 615 persons respectively and comprised 748 POW – the majority aboard the *Letitia* – and 856 civilian internees. To these were added another 3,400, or thereabouts, crammed aboard the *Arundel Castle* at Liverpool.

The *Letitia* set out from Falmouth on 26 December 1944 bound for Halifax, Nova Scotia, where she arrived during the night of 2–3 January 1945 to pick up seventy-one POW who had been held in a Canadian prison camp. She left Halifax on 4 January and docked at Pier D, Jersey City, two days later. After embarkation aboard her and the *Gripsholm* was complete, they sailed together on 7 January, heading direct for the Mediterranean.

Following her participation in the Gothenburg exchange in September 1944, the *Arundel Castle* was engaged for a second mission to Marseilles in January 1945 supported by the hospital ship *Letitia*, seen here at Liverpool. *Author's collection*

Eight days later, the *Arundel Castle* departed Liverpool, sailing independently. According to the recollections of former crew members, she was not painted with any safe-passage markings on this occasion. Nor, they say, was she temporarily disarmed, though how this would have accorded with her safe-conduct status cannot be clarified. She arrived off Gibraltar on 18 January where she rendezvoused with the *Gripsholm* and *Letitia* the following day. On 20 January, the three ships continued their voyage together, pulling in to Marseilles the next day.

Because the actual transfer of repatriates was taking place at Kreuzlingen, the *Arundel Castle*, *Gripsholm* and *Letitia* were required to remain in port for longer. The first two trains left Marseilles for Lausanne and Zurich on the day of the arrival. More followed, all of them reaching Kreuzlingen during 23 and 24 January. Most of the personnel they carried continued into Germany via Konstanz, but others, presumably of Austrian origin, were transported by train to Bregenz. Meanwhile, the Allied repatriates, who had crossed the border from Germany some days earlier, were moved to St Gallen where they waited to make the return rail journey to Marseilles. They were a mix of POW and civilian concentration camp internees, including some arrested war correspondents treated as POW, approximately 2,500 in total. Among them were 713 American civilians, less than the expected number by 162. To make up the difference, another forty-six US citizens who had been held in Bergen-Belsen concentration camp were added, plus a number of Poles and ten Latin Americans suffering from various illnesses, raising the total to 826. As these supplementary individuals were destined for the *Gripsholm* and took time to assemble, her sojourn at Marseilles proved to be the longest.

After taking aboard the repatriates, the three Allied ships headed home, beginning with the *Letitia*, which left Marseilles on 24 January, passed Gibraltar on 26 January and docked at Liverpool on 1 February. Twelve days later she returned to Halifax, arriving on 22 February to deliver the Canadian contingent of the returned POW. The *Arundel Castle* sailed on 29 January, disembarked at Liverpool on 5 February and was then repositioned at Gourock.

It was not until well after the two British ships had returned to the UK that the *Gripsholm* finally made her departure from Marseilles. She sailed on 8 February following a circuitous route in the Mediterranean before crossing the Atlantic. She called at Port Said, Alexandria, Haifa, Piraeus, Naples and Palermo, finally arriving at Jersey City on 25 February 1945. In so doing she ended her wartime career as a repatriation mercy ship. However, the *Gripsholm* remained under charter to the US Government until 1946, assisting in the post-war repatriation of American troops from around the world as part of Operation *Magic Carpet*.

Colour photographs of mercy ships, in fact of most merchant ships, from the Second World War period are rare indeed. Here the *Duilio* is seen at Trieste during preparations prior to her first repatriation mission, painted in the colour scheme that was devised for these operations. *Horst Gründ, courtesy of Bündesarchiv*

An impression of the *Asama Maru* as a wartime transport. For the July 1942 exchange at Lourenço Marques she was painted in the same colours as the *Conte Verde*, shown in the next picture. *Kihachiro Ueda*

Conte Verde –1942.

Starboard side elevation of the *Conte Verde*, exhibiting the colour scheme adopted for her, the *Asama Maru* and *Tatuta Maru*. *Paolo Valenti*

Another impression of a wartime Japanese transport, the *Teia Maru* ex *Aramis*. Her exchange mission colours were the same as those in which the *Awa Maru* was painted. *Kihachiro Ueda*

Another rare wartime colour photograph, in this case of the hospital ship
Letitia, No. 66. *Library & Archives of Canada/Department of National
Defence*

Before selection for her unique mercy mission, the *Awa Maru* served as an
armed transport with the Imperial Japanese Navy. *Kihachiro Ueda*

The *Awa Maru* sinking, illustrating the alternative Japanese protective colour scheme as also applied to the *Teia Maru* and *Kamakura Maru*. This imaginary portrayal of her loss could never have been seen because she was sunk at night in thick fog. *Global Books*

The *Gripsholm* in Swedish neutrality markings. *Curt Dawe, courtesy of Sjöfartsmuseet Akvariet*

An artist's impression of the *Lillie Matthiessen* in Swedish neutrality colours. *Jan Goedhardt*

The *Arundel Castle* at Cape Town post-war. *Ian Shiffman*

Following a major refit and modification, the *Città di Tunisi* re-emerged with a new funnel and more modern exterior styling. Compare this picture with the one of her on page 28. *Mario Cicogna*

Swedish America Line had the *Gripsholm* rebuilt from 1949 during which she received new funnels and a raked bow, which increased her length to 590ft. In 1955 she was sold to Norddeutscher Lloyd and became the *Berlin*. *Kenneth W. Wightman*

After her return to her owners in 1946, the *Oranje* switched to a round-the-world service. She later became the much-altered *Angelina Lauro. Don Liem*

After the war, the *Rio Jachál* was returned to SGTM and reverted to her original name, *Campana.* In June 1955 she was sold to Sicula Oceanica and renamed *Irpinia* for the Genoa to Central America service. From 1962 her twin funnels were replaced with a single one of more modern style. *Richard de Kerbrech*

Like the *Saturnia*, sister ship *Vulcania* was restored to Italia Line's transatlantic service from Trieste to New York until she was sold to Sicula Oceanica in 1965. She is seen here berthed at New York. *Author's collection*

At the end of her war service, the *West Point* was returned to the United States Lines and restored to her original name, *America*. This photograph was taken during a call at Southampton. *Kenneth W. Wightman*

Mission 27: Singapore, March 1945

Much has been written about the loss of the safe-conduct ship *Awa Maru* and the circumstances in which she was sunk. Her inclusion here is because, primarily, hers *was* one of the relief missions of the Second World War conducted under the auspices of the ICRC, but also to illustrate how the war hazard to which she succumbed with its tragic consequences was one that potentially faced all mercy ships. Luckily, though, of all the passenger-carrying mercy ships she was the sole victim of a mistaken attack.

In many respects, her mission was also unique. It did not involve an exchange of repatriates, nor was it a case of a one-sided repatriation, as in the case of the four Italian liners that conveyed internees held by the British from East Africa in 1942 and 1943 (Missions 7, 12 and 17). In her case, the mission had been arranged primarily to permit the distribution of urgently needed Red Cross parcels to Allied POW suffering severe deprivation in Japanese prison camps across China and South East Asia. As one of the concessions for making this vital humanitarian voyage, the *Awa Maru* was permitted to take Japanese non-combatant citizens back to Japan from Japanese-occupied Singapore under international safe-conduct guarantees. Hence, when she left Singapore for Japan on 28 March 1945, she was carrying in excess of 2,000 passengers and crew.

Prior to the voyage, negotiations with Japan through the Swiss Government in Geneva and its legation in Tokyo had been endeavouring for some months to secure an agreement for a parcel drop, expecting Japan to abide by its declared commitment to support the provision of food and healthcare to the prisoners it held. Tragically, however, the reality was very different. When, finally, an agreement was reached for a relief voyage, the US Government and American Red Cross arranged for a large quantity of parcels to be deposited in the Russian port of Nakhodka for collection in November 1944 by a Japanese freighter, the *Hakusan Maru*. On reaching Japan, these supplies were split partly between the *Hoshi Maru*, another cargo ship, to be taken to Shanghai, with a quantity retained for distribution within the Japanese home islands and the remainder, around 2,000 tons, destined for the *Awa Maru*.

Demilitarised and painted in the declared Japanese safe-passage colours, the *Awa Maru* sailed from Moji on 17 February 1945. Her southbound route took her to Taka, Formosa (now Taiwan) on 20 February, Hong Kong (22–23 February), Saigon (25–28 February) and Singapore where she arrived on 2 March. So far, so good. After six days in port, the *Awa Maru* commenced a delivery circuit in the Java Sea. Her first call was at Batavia (now Jakarta) from 10–18 March, after which she made for Muntok on Banka Belitung Island, off the coast of Sumatra (19–20 March). A scheduled call at Surabaya was omitted. She returned

As part of her mission, the *Awa Maru* was conveying Red Cross parcels and other humanitarian aid to Allied prisoners held by the Japanese in camps across the southern Pacific and South East Asia. The *Hakusan Maru*, seen here, was deployed to collect those vital materials from Nakhodka in the Soviet Union and take them to the *Awa Maru*, waiting at Moji. *Arnold Kludas*

to Singapore on 24 March and proceeded to embark 1,923 passengers. With her crew of 148, her entire complement therefore was 2,071.

Four days later, at 1000 hours local time, she departed for Japan, the intention being to head direct to Moji, making no calls at interim ports. Her route through the South China Sea would take her close to the coast of Malaya and Vietnam, then through the Formosa Strait into the East China Sea. But she never got that far.

As required, she transmitted her noon position on each day of the voyage, the last message broadcast on 1 April placing her north-east of Swatow (now Shantou) in the position 23.20N, 117.27E. She was also maintaining a steady course, keeping to the plotted route, and in darkness her markings were fully illuminated and her running lights switched on. But the weather was not favourable, with visibility down to 200 yards, making her difficult to see, despite these measures.

On patrol in the area of the Formosa Strait was the US submarine *Queenfish* under the command of Charles Elliott Loughlin, which, at the time, was experiencing radio reception problems. COMSUBPAC repeatedly broadcast a message in plain language regarding the safe-conduct status of the *Awa Maru* both prior to the outbound voyage and prior to her return, giving a description of the ship, her route and itinerary. Partly because of the reception problems, partly due to a higher priority being given to encrypted messages over those in plain language, and partly due to irregularities in the procedures followed by the submarine's radio operators, the messages never reached the *Queenfish's* commander. Nor had the *Awa Maru* been mentioned during the pre-sortie Staff Officer's briefing at Saipan in February 1945. When, finally, a message concerning the *Awa Maru* was picked up by the *Queenfish*, it failed to provide the relief ship's route or the sea areas through which she would be passing. It simply bracketed the dates of her return voyage as being from 30 March to 4 April, which were, in fact, incorrect.

The dice were loaded and about to be cast. In ignorance of the whereabouts of the *Awa Maru* and unable to see her clearly in the dense sea fog, the *Queenfish's* commander inevitably treated as hostile the ship that first showed up as a blip on his radar screen at around 2300 hours on 1 April 1945. Failing to associate the radar signal's characteristics – steady speed of 16 knots on a straight course – with the *Awa Maru*, it was deduced instead that, with a low radar signature, the target must be a Japanese destroyer and an attack was launched.

Struck by four torpedoes evenly spread along her length, the *Awa Maru* did not stand a chance and sank within four minutes, taking all but a very few of her occupants with her. When one of these occupants, Kantora Shimoda – who was believed to be, but not confirmed as, the sole survivor – was pulled from the sea, the calamitous error was revealed. The lives of well over 2,000 persons had been lost, all of whom had probably been unprepared for any sort of emergency evacuation, no matter how short the opportunity, believing they were reasonably secure sailing under safe-conduct protection.

In the wake of the disaster, Commander Loughlin was tried by a military court for culpable inefficiency, disobeying a lawful order and negligence. His punishment took the form of an official admonishment, which may or may not have been appropriate given the gravity of the consequences of his actions. The greater concern, though, was how Japan would react.

Although the war against Japan was being won, there was no knowing when it would end. Until it did, American and Allied POW, who the Japanese had steadfastly refused to repatriate, would continue to suffer at the hands of their captors, so America was anxious to have relief voyages continue. Japan lodged protests in the strongest possible terms and the Americans acknowledged their responsibility for the sinking with an apology of sorts, but the fact was there were no more relief voyages for Allied POW before the end of the war on 2 September 1945.

Apart from cancellations and debates over their constituent repatriates, none of the mercy missions experienced major problems or, despite the attendant risks, calamitous outcomes. That was until the *Awa Maru* made her fateful voyage under protected status to Singapore in the spring of 1945. This photograph purportedly shows the *Awa Maru* as an Imperial Japanese Navy transport, but it has also been captioned as the *Aki Maru*, one of the *Awa Maru*'s sisters. *Nippon Yusen Kaisha*

Mission 28: Gothenburg, March 1945 and Istanbul, April 1945

On 8 March 1945, the *Drottningholm* embarked on her last and longest wartime repatriation mission. By the time it ended, the war in Europe had been over by almost a month. Unlike her earlier missions, for this repatriation voyage she was chartered by the German Government, the prime purpose being the exchange of diplomats with Turkey and the Lebanon. Turkey's valuable role as a neutral intermediary had ended when it broke off diplomatic relations with Nazi Germany and then, on 23 February 1945, declared war.

Through the offices of the Swiss Government and the ICRC, Germany and Turkey immediately negotiated for the mutual return of their diplomats and other officials. However, as Switzerland had now also become more difficult to reach, a mission would need to take place by sea, passing through waters controlled by the British and requiring safe-conduct guarantees from the British Government. Britain was not averse to such a repatriation being performed but chose to take advantage of the situation by demanding in exchange for the granting of safe-passage that more British captives should be released, principally the Channel Islanders who had been removed to forced labour in Germany in September 1942. Arising from that concession, the British became, at 350, the largest group of *Drottningholm*'s passengers. The others were 325 Turkish citizens, among them forty Turkish Jews from Holland and eighty officials from the Turkish Embassy in Berlin; 130 Swedes, diplomats, missionaries and businessmen; and around thirty of either Portuguese or Peruvian nationality. Last, but certainly not least, there were 115 Argentine subjects, the diplomats who had been denied repatriation from Lisbon to Buenos Aires the previous August (Mission 24). There was also a Swedish doctor and nurse, plus six Red Cross medical assistants to care for sixty of the British repatriates who were extremely ill.

Although Gothenburg had been reinstated as the embarkation port – it was not the exchange port because the *Drottningholm* was to take Allied repatriates outbound and return with the exchanged Germans from Istanbul – there were complications with regard to the means of getting her intended passengers from Germany to Sweden.

Confronting a total collapse of its forces in the east as the Red Army advanced into Pomerania, Silesia and Prussia, Operation *Hannibal* had been launched in January 1945 to rescue as many trapped German citizens as possible and take them to the relative safety of the west. Allocated to the operation, along with hundreds of other vessels, were the *Meteor*, *Rügen* and the train ferry *Deutschland*. The *Meteor* was bombed and sunk at Pillau (now Baltiysk) on 9 March 1945 and eight days later the *Deutschland* was captured by the Soviets. The absence and loss of these ships removed the transportation capability between Swinemünde and Gothenburg and probably also between Sassnitz and Trelleborg. It is possible, though it cannot be confirmed, that the *Drottning Victoria* assisted by her sister ship *Konung Gustav V* transferred some of the repatriates by the latter route, but the majority were conveyed across the land border with Denmark to Padborg, 5 miles north of Flensburg, where there was a holding camp. From Padborg they crossed on ferries, first from Svendborg to Korsør and then from Copenhagen to Malmö.

After leaving Gothenburg, the *Drottningholm* cleared Kristiansand (16–18 March) and British Contraband Control in the Faeroes (20 March). At Liverpool on 23 March her British passengers disembarked and at her next port of call, Lisbon, the 115 Argentine diplomats were landed on 28 March. From Lisbon she sailed the length of the Mediterranean to Port Said where she stayed for two days (4–5 April). Next, she made for Istanbul where she arrived on 8 April. At Istanbul, after the last of her outward repatriates had been landed, the German diplomats from the embassies in Ankara and Beirut were embarked, 358 in total. Fifty-seven Swiss, twenty-three Swedes, two Portuguese and one Spanish citizen also boarded the ship.

Having been chartered previously by the United States and Great Britain, the *Drottningholm*'s final and possibly most complex mercy mission was performed under charter to Germany. *Sjöfartsmuseet Akvariet*

The *Drottningholm* left Istanbul on 21 April, called at Lisbon (1–9 May) and Liverpool (12–28 May) and finally reached Gothenburg at the end of the voyage on 4 June 1945. No information has been found to explain the long duration of the calls made at Lisbon and Liverpool. Thereafter, under charter to the Ministry of War Transport from 26 July 1945 to 2 March 1946, the *Drottningholm* continued to assist in the repatriation of British troops from different parts of the world, but for her the wartime mercy exploits were finally over.

Missions 29 and 30: Lübeck, April 1945 and June–July 1945

The final Red Cross mission of the Second World War was implemented from June to July 1945, after the war in Europe had ended. It was a triumph that earned Sweden much goodwill and it endorsed Sweden's deserved reputation as a nation with high humanitarian standards, values that have remained associated with it ever since.

Arising from Sweden's successful execution of the 'White Buses' operation, as it was called in the closing days of the war, from March to May 1945, the United

Nations Relief and Rehabilitation Administration (UNRRA) appealed to the Swedish Government on behalf of the victorious Allies to consider implementing a second repatriation of displaced concentration camp survivors who urgently needed care and refuge.

The Allied military forces, preoccupied with stabilising the situation in a devastated and broken Germany and the rounding up of Nazi war criminals who remained at large, were unable to adequately provide the medical aid, sustenance and post-traumatic care required by the thousands who had been fortunate enough to survive.

The 'White Buses' operation had been initiated and launched by Sweden with the backing and involvement of the ICRC. It was later supported by the Danish and Norwegian authorities in a bid to rescue as many of the endangered internees as possible still held in the concentration camps – not to return them to their home countries but to take them to safety and protective rehabilitation in Sweden as an interim measure. At the end of 1944, Germany was on the brink of military collapse and political chaos, circumstances that, on the one hand, exacerbated the threat facing surviving captives but, on the other, permitted Sweden to push for concessions from the Nazi hierarchy that, barely a year earlier, would have been beyond contemplation.

As the war drew to a close and the threatened Nazi hierarchy became ever more desperate, the lives of countless concentration camp inmates were exposed to yet more dangers. Some at least benefitted from the so-called 'White Buses' humanitarian initiative instigated jointly by Sweden and Denmark with the support of the Norwegian authorities and the full involvement of the ICRC. Among the ships that carried survivors to Sweden was the Sven Sálen refrigerated cargo ship *Lillie Matthiessen. Sjöfartsmuseet Akvariet*

Primarily an overland operation, because Germany would at first only permit the transfer of prisoners to Denmark rather than Sweden, ultimately, towards the end of the mission, some mercy crossings by sea became essential in order to complete the task. The Sven Sálen cargo ships *Lillie Matthiessen* and *Magdalena*, which had brought fuel and emergency relief supplies to Lübeck, were hastily co-opted as passenger-carriers and they sailed together from Lübeck to Malmö on 30 April transporting approximately 300 and 550 internees respectively. Earlier, from 16–18 April, another unnamed ship had taken 423 Danish Jews to Sweden by the same route.

The remarkable 'White Buses' operation, impressive in its scale though logistically challenging, ultimately conveyed 15,345 persons (the authenticated Swedish Red Cross figure) to safety and restorative care in Sweden, the greatest number rescued from Nazi Germany during the war in a single humanitarian exercise. Just over half were Scandinavians, mainly Danes and Swedes, the others, numbering 7,550, were a mix of French, Dutch and Polish.

Both Britain and the United States endorsed the mission. However, they were unable to guarantee safety for the volunteer-manned road convoys from air attack, some comprising as many as 114 buses and other vehicles as they penetrated deep into Germany to collect internees from the dispersed camps where they were held. It was the British Government that recommended having the buses painted white with prominent red crosses to assist in their recognition.

With the fronts closing in rapidly on Germany and fighting taking place on its own soil, the operation had to be wound up after nine weeks, and the last bus convoy of the expedition left Neuengamme for Padborg on 25 April 1945. The last ferry with internees crossed from Copenhagen to Malmö nine days later, three days before Germany capitulated.

Given the accomplishments of the 'White Buses' operation and the fact that neutral Sweden was relatively close by and its infrastructure remained intact, it was the obvious choice when it was deemed that a follow-on humanitarian mission to aid thousands of homeless, hungry refugees was needed immediately post-war. In this instance a seaborne operation was the preference, as it had probably been, had it been permitted, for the earlier operation.

To its credit, the Swedish Government fully comprehended the urgency of the situation and that quick decisions were called for following the UNRRA approach. Within a day, on 1 June 1945, it announced its consent to undertake the mission and promptly commenced detailed planning for the 'Humanitarian Service', as it was called. It is hard to imagine the utter state of collapse and breakdown of order that accompanied the end of the Third Reich. Despite sterling efforts by overwhelmed British medical teams at Bergen-Belsen, 13,994 liberated internees had died of typhus, tuberculosis and malnutrition at that camp alone between the end of April and the end of June. To contain the epidemic, in the absence of quarantine facilities, it was imperative to get those who were uninfected away. It was decided that a minimum of five ships was required for the mission: the Swedish Navy ship *Prins Carl* and four chartered vessels requisitioned by the Swedish Maritime Administration, the small passenger ships *Kastelholm* and *Kronprinsessan Ingrid*, and the cargo ships *Karskär* and *Rönnskär*.

Without delay, the ships were prepared for their special role and their regular crews were supplemented by volunteers recruited from the Swedish Civil Defence Board and the Red Cross, along with a sizeable medical team. Although the war had ended, it was considered expedient for the chartered vessels to be painted white with Red Cross markings, and also their names and Swedish nationality, to indicate that they were on an ICRC-mandated mission and were protected ships. The Baltic Sea was still a dangerous place, besides which the Russians were reluctant to support all the Allied initiatives. They were known to be hostile to releases of some former prisoners in case wanted Nazis slipped through the net among them, and there was a risk of intervention.

To manage the operation at the German end, a preliminary detachment of volunteers was dispatched on 19 June to Lübeck, the only German port that was still functional. The same day, the first train with 400 ex-inmates set off from Bergen-Belsen to Lübeck. The mercy ships set out on their inaugural crossings from Trelleborg on 22 and 23 June. They headed first to Travemünde where they were joined by a German minesweeper, which escorted them along the coast to Lübeck.

One of the units of the 'Humanitarian Service', as it was called, was the small Swedish America coastal passenger ship *Kastelholm*. *Britt Bjorkdal, courtesy of Morgan Lundberg*

After embarking their passengers, the ships sailed from Lübeck to various Swedish ports that had been designated and equipped as reception points – Malmö, Kalmar, Norrköping and Stockholm. Over the next month, until the mission ended on 26 July 1945, the ships crossed back and forth, making a total of thirty-six round trips. By that time, 9,273 persons, the majority women but also some children, had been evacuated and were receiving treatment in the medical and sanitary centres that had been set up at Ropsten, east of Uppsala, Småland, inland from Stockholm, Ramlösa, south-east of Helsingborg and Fröslov, east of Ystad. Some of the worst cases were still there three years later.

The 'White Buses' operation remains a lasting legacy to Count Folke Bernadotte of Wisborg, the Vice-President of the Swedish Red Cross, who, through various relief efforts, helped save the lives of countless concentration camp internees and vigorously promoted humanitarian intervention. Perhaps the greatest tribute to him and his Swedish countrymen, though, was a revised Geneva Convention, inspired by them and fittingly agreed in Stockholm in 1948 to be ratified a year

The *Kronprinsessan Ingrid* displaying Swedish Red Cross markings passes through the Falsterbö Canal bound for Malmö. *Berndt Johnsson*

One of two cargo ships that served in the 'Humanitarian Service' fleet was the *Karskär*. *Alex Duncan*

later, which provided for the rights of protection in wartime of captured civilians and military prisoners. Today, the House of Humanity also stands in Malmö as a lasting memorial to the 'White Buses' operation, the 'Humanitarian Service', Count Bernadotte and all the wartime humanitarian work of the Swedish Red Cross and Swedish people.

Postscript

Given the huge numbers of prisoners-of-war incarcerated around the globe during the Second World War and the equally vast count of civilians that were held captive in concentration and internment camps, it might reasonably be argued that the endeavours of the mercy ships were no more than a scratch on the surface. But in a conflict as savage and brutal as the Second World War, engulfing every level of humanity, any and every effort that helped to save life, no matter how small, had to be worthwhile.

In total, the repatriations and exchanges undertaken by the mercy ships accounted for the liberation and removal to safety of approximately 150,000 persons. The *Gripsholm* alone ferried 27,712 repatriates over her six mercy voyages, while a post-war Italian report states that a total of 27,726 persons were repatriated by the four liners over the course of the three East African missions. And Sweden's 'White Buses' operation and the 'Humanitarian Service' together accounted for over 24,500. By any reckoning these were major achievements, which, in the annals of the war, deserve greater approbation.

Merchant seamen in general from the Second World War have received scant recognition for their huge contribution in maintaining vital supplies of food and other essential commodities, besides serving in various auxiliary capacities for the duration. Equally, there has been little official acknowledgement, other than in Sweden and the USA, of the exceptional work of the mercy ship crews who bravely, and in some cases voluntarily, undertook their duties in the face of considerable danger, trusting totally on their safe-conduct status being universally respected. It speaks volumes that the passengers on virtually every one of these ships recalled that the crews exhibited cheerfulness, hospitality and fortitude in the fulfilment of their duties.

3

THE FATES AND SUBSEQUENT CAREERS OF THE MERCY SHIPS

AQUILEIA

15 December 1943: attacked and set on fire by Allied aircraft at Marseilles, left in a flooded condition, resting on the seabed. **February 1944**: raised and undergoing repairs. **26 June 1944**: deliberately scuttled by the retreating German forces; raised a second time after the war but assessed as beyond viable restoration and demolished.

ARGENTINA

September 1943: seized by the Germans. **13 October 1943**: captured by the Royal Navy; requisitioned as a personnel ship under British India Line management. **1946**: returned to Tirrenia Line and resumed Mediterranean ferry service. **August 1960**: disposed of for breaking up at Genoa.

The *Argentina* resumed passenger service post-war, once again making regular calls at Valletta. *Michael Cassar*

ARUNDEL CASTLE

1947: released to Union-Castle Line; used for emigrant service to Cape Town. **September 1950**: resumed Southampton–Cape Town mail service. **December 1958**: final departure from Southampton bound for Kowloon to be broken up.

ASAMA MARU

1 November 1944: torpedoed and sunk by USS *Atule* in the China Sea, 100 miles south of Pratos Island, in the position 20.17N, 117.08E, while bound from Manila to Takao in convoy MAMO-04.

ATLANTIS

1948: released to Royal Mail Line; refurbished for emigrant voyages to Australia and New Zealand. **1952**: sold for breaking up at Faslane.

Another mercy ship seen post-war, the *Atlantis*. *Newall Dunn collection*

CABO DE BUENA ESPERANZA

1945: resumed Barcelona–La Plata ports scheduled service. **September 1958**: arrived at Barcelona for breaking up.

CABO DE HORNOS

1945: resumed Barcelona–La Plata ports scheduled service. **22 February 1959**: arrived at Aviles for breaking up.

CALITEA

June 1940: employed as a troopship. **11 December 1941**: torpedoed and sunk by HMS *Talisman*, 90 miles south of Cape Matapan, in the position 36.23N, 20.33E.

CITTÀ DI TUNISI

September 1943: captured by the Germans and renamed *Heidelberg*. **1944**: damaged in Allied air attacks and abandoned at San Rocco by retreating German forces. **February 1946**: recovered and restored; deployed as a troopship. **April 1947**: returned to Tirrenia Line. **3 June 1947**: resumed Naples–Palermo–Tunis passenger service. **1951–1952**: modernised at Naples during winter overhaul. **Late 1950s**: Naples–Reggio Calabria–Catania–Syracuse–Valletta–Tripoli service. **1970**: Naples–Cagliari–Palermo service. **16 November 1970**: left Naples for breaking up at Trieste.

The *City of Canterbury*
following alterations after
the end of her war service.
Author's collection

CITY OF CANTERBURY

October 1942: resumed troop ferrying. **1947**: returned to Ellerman Lines, resumed London–Beira service. **31 May 1953**: arrived at Blyth to be broken up.

CITY OF PARIS

October 1942: resumed troop ferrying. **1944**: accommodation ship. **1945**: resumed troopship service. **1947**: returned to Ellerman Lines; refitted and overhauled at Newcastle before resuming London–Africa service. **24 February 1956**: arrived at Newport, Monmouthshire (now Gwent) for demolition.

CONTE ROSSO

August 1940: service as a troopship. **24 May 1941**: torpedoed and sunk east of Syracuse, in the position 36.41N, 15.42E, by HMS *Upholder*.

CONTE VERDE

September 1942: returned to lay-up, moored off the Bund at Shanghai. **11 September 1943**: scuttled by her crew; refloated by the Japanese and taken to Maizuru for repairs and conversion into a troopship; renamed *Kotobuki Maru* although there was no physical evidence of a name change. **December 1944**: damaged in US air raids. **8 May 1945**: bombed and sunk in Nakata Bay in position 34.30N, 126.30E. **June 1949**: refloated and dry-docked. **1950**: ownership reverted to the Italian Government but wreck remained in Japan. **1951**: broken up at Maizuru.

The wreck of the *Conte Verde* in dry dock awaiting a decision on her future. As she was beyond recovery she was broken up locally. *Author's collection*

Late in the war, the *Cuba* succumbed to a U-boat torpedo and sank south of the Isle of Wight on 20 April 1945. *Author's collection*

CUBA

November 1943: resumed troopship service. **6 April 1945**: torpedoed and sunk by U1195 50 miles south of the Isle of Wight while bound Le Havre–Southampton.

DEUTSCHLAND

January 1945: attached to Operation *Hannibal* evacuating refugees from East Prussia to Denmark. **17 March 1945**: seized by the Russians; renamed *Orion* for Black Sea service; subsequently transferred for operation in the Far East by Sovietsky Zhelesny Doroga Parokhodstvo. **1946**: renamed *Aniva*; reconditioned and modified with a single rounded-top funnel. **1959**: scrapped following an accident.

DINARD

23 May 1945: returned to Southampton at the end of her hospital carrier service; refitted at London. **October 1945**: troopship service Newhaven–Dieppe. **24 May 1946**: troopship service Tilbury–Antwerp. **15 June 1946**: troopship service Dover–Calais, then returned to Southern Railway. **1 July 1947**: car ferry service Dover–Boulogne. **1948**: absorbed into the nationalised British

Transport Commission fleet as a British Railways Southern Region ship. **1959**: sold to Rederi A/B Vikinglinjen, Mariehamn, for service in the Baltic; renamed *Viking*. **1970**: withdrawn from service. **16 October 1973**: arrived at Helsinki for breaking up.

Another ship that underwent a major transformation after the war was Compagnie de Navigation Paquet's *Djenné*. *Skyfotos*

DJENNÉ

26 August 1944: scuttled by the Germans at Marseilles. **26 August 1946**: refloated; restored for recommencement of commercial service. **7 August 1948**: resumed Marseilles–Tangier–Casablanca service for Paquet Line. **1952**: underwent a major overhaul. **September 1962**: transferred to Compagnie de Navigation and renamed *Caesarea*. **1964**: withdrawn from service. **May 1966**: arrived at Split, Yugoslavia, for demolition.

DROTTNINGHOLM

1946: declared surplus to Swedish America Line requirements; sold to Home Lines, the transaction completed in 1948; renamed *Brasil*. **27 July 1948**: Genoa–South America service. **1950**: Naples–New York service. **1951**: renamed *Homeland*. **16 June 1951**: Hamburg–New York service. **1952**: Genoa–New York service. **29 March 1955**: arrived at Trieste for breaking up.

The *Drottningholm* was sold soon after the Second World War to Home Lines. Initially renamed *Brasil*, from 1951 she became the *Homeland*. *G.E.P. Brownell courtesy of World Ship Society*

Having resumed full trans-Baltic service in 1945, the *Drottning Victoria* underwent reconstruction and modernisation in 1953. Note her broader funnels. *World Ship Society*

DROTTNING VICTORIA

1945–1946: re-entered cross-Baltic train ferry service, opening new routes from Trelleborg to Gdansk and Gdynia. **1953**: modernised during refit. **1968**: paid off for disposal. **1969**: broken up at Ystad.

DUILIO

10 July 1944: sunk at an anchorage at Vallone di Zaule, near San Sabbia, Muggia, south of Trieste, during an Allied air raid. **11 September 1944**: wreck sustained more damage in another air raid. **1948**: wreck raised. **11 February 1948**: demolition commenced at San Rocco.

British aircraft target the *Duilio* at her anchorage near Trieste. *Author's collection*

EL NIL

1943: converted into Hospital Ship 53 at New York; between 1943 and 1946 became the property of the British Government. **1946**: troopship service for Ministry of Transport but retained hospital ship facilities and personnel. **1950**: laid up on the River Clyde. **April 1951**: sold to the Pan-Islamic Steamship Co., Pakistan, for pilgrim voyages across the Indian Ocean to Saudi Arabia; renamed *Safina-E-Murad*. **October 1952**: laid up. **4 January 1953**: arrived at Karachi for breaking up.

EMPRESS OF RUSSIA

8 September 1945: during repairs and refit at Vickers-Armstrongs at Barrow-in-Furness she caught fire and was completely gutted. **1946**: the burnt-out hulk demolished at Barrow.

In September 1945, while undergoing restoration at Barrow-in-Furness, the *Empress of Russia* caught fire. Her wreck was demolished locally. *Author's collection*

GIULIO CESARE

25 August 1944: extensively damaged during an Allied air raid on the anchorage at Vallone di Zaule, near San Sabbia, Muggia, south of Trieste. **11 September 1944**: after further air attacks, she rolled over onto her starboard side, coming to rest partially submerged in shallow water. **1949**: the wreck raised and demolished locally.

The *Giulio Cesare* lies on her side near Trieste after she was bombed. *Mario Cicogna*

GRADISCA

May 1945: taken as a war prize and became a British troopship. **2 January 1946**: stranded off the island of Gavdhos, near Crete, while bound Port Said–Malta. **June 1947**: refloated, towed to Venice and laid up. **1949**: scrapped locally.

GRIPSHOLM

March 1946: returned to regular Swedish America Line transatlantic passenger service. **1949–1950**: underwent reconstruction and a major overhaul at the Howaldtswerke shipyard, Kiel. **1 February 1954**: Bremerhaven–Southampton–New York service for Bremen-America Line, a joint venture with Norddeutscher Lloyd. **January 1955**: acquired by Norddeutscher Lloyd and renamed *Berlin*. **26 November 1966**: arrived at La Spezia for breaking up.

KAMAKURA MARU

28 April 1943: torpedoed and sunk by USS *Gudgeon* east of Palawan, in the Sulu Sea, in the position 10.25N, 121.44E, while on passage Manila-Singapore.

KASTELHOLM

1952: sold to Ångfartygs Ab Mariehamn for Åbo-Mariehamn–Stockholm service. **1954**: sold to Ångfartygs Ab Bore for Åbo-Köpenhamn cruises calling at Visby, Rönne and Stockholm. **1972**: sold to Ångfartygs Ab Strömma Kanal, subsequently passing briefly to other owners. **August 1975**: broken up at Ystad.

KRONPRINSESSAN INGRID

1955: sold to Gotland Ångfartygs and renamed *Christofer Polhem*. **1963**: sold to C. Hogberg and renamed *Marina*. **2006**: retired from service and presumed broken up.

LETITIA

1946: sold to British Government for service as an MoT troopship; renamed *Empire Brent*. **1950**: emigrant service Glasgow–Sydney. **5 February 1952**: emigrant service Glasgow–Wellington, New Zealand via Panama; acquired by New Zealand Government and renamed *Captain Cook*. **1955**: Glasgow–Montreal service. **October 1955**: resumed Glasgow–Wellingon service. **February 1960**: laid up at Falmouth. **29 April 1960**: arrived at Inverkeithing for breaking up.

LILLIE MATTHIESSEN

1951: transferred within Sven Salén to Rederi A/B Pulp. **6 June 1952**: arrived at Hemixem, Belgium, for breaking up.

LLANDOVERY CASTLE

September 1946: released to Union-Castle Line. **May 1947**: resumed London–round Africa service. **11 December 1952**: arrived at Inverkeithing for breaking up.

METEOR [II]

9 March 1945: bombed and sunk during an air raid at Pillau (now Baltiysk) while engaged transporting refugees in Operation *Hannibal*.

MONARCH OF BERMUDA

24 March 1947: severely damaged by fire during post-war renovation at Newcastle; the wreck was purchased by the Ministry of Transport for reconstruction as an emigrant carrier by Thornycroft at Southampton. **1949**: renamed *New Australia*. **15 August 1950**: entered Southampton–Sydney migrant service managed by Shaw, Savill & Albion. **January 1958**: sold to Greek Line; renamed *Arkadia*. **22 May 1958**: entered Bremerhaven–Montreal service calling at either Tilbury or Southampton. **18 December 1966**: arrived at Valencia for breaking up.

Following a fire at Newcastle on 24 March 1947, which almost destroyed her, the *Monarch of Bermuda* was rebuilt as the emigrant ship *New Australia*. Note that her aft funnel has been removed while the forward funnel has been modified as a combined exhaust and foremast. *Mick Lindsay*

NARKUNDA

13 November 1942: torpedoed by the Italian submarine *Platino* while leaving Bougie bound for Algiers during the Operation *Torch* landings in North Africa; bombed, set on fire and sunk the following day in the position 36.49N, 05.01E.

NEWFOUNDLAND

13 September 1943: struck by an aircraft-launched missile and caught fire during the Salerno landings. **14 September 1943**: damage was so extreme, she was towed further out to sea and scuttled in the position 40.13N, 14.21E.

ORANJE

July 1946: returned to Nederland Line and re-entered the Amsterdam–Batavia service. **1950**: Amsterdam–Panama–Auckland–Sydney–Singapore–Suez–Amsterdam round-the-world service with occasional calls at Southampton. **September 1964**: sold to Achille Lauro and renamed *Angelina Lauro*; completely rebuilt at the Cantieri del Tirreno shipyard, Genoa – extensive structural alterations left her unrecognisable. **6 March 1966**: Bremerhaven–London–Wellington service. **1968**: Southampton–Sydney service. **1972**: full-time cruising. **18 September 1976**: laid up at La Spezia. **October 1977**: commenced three-year charter to Costa Armatori SpA and renamed *Angelina*; later reverted to *Angelina Lauro*. **30 March 1979**: gutted by fire at Charlotte Amalie, St Thomas; flooded and settled on seabed. **June 1979**: refloated and towed away for breaking up at Taiwan. **24 September 1979**: sank between Panama and Hawaii in the position 11.44N, 121.43W.

Seen at Port Said in 1947, the *Orduña* went on to survive for another three years, employed carrying troops for the British Government. *David Wilcockson*

ORDUÑA

February 1941: requisitioned as a troopship. **November 1950**: final trooping voyage, Singapore–Liverpool. **1951**: scrapped at Dalmuir.

PRESIDENT COOLIDGE

26 October 1942: struck an American mine while approaching Espiritu Santo, New Hebrides (now Vanuatu), from Nouméa, New Caledonia; beached but rolled over onto her port side and sank.

The *President Coolidge* met her end under a year after the United States' entry into the war when she struck a 'friendly' mine at Espiritu Santo, Vanuatu, on 26 October 1942. All but five of her 5,000 occupants were saved. *US Navy*

RIO JÁCHAL

1946: returned to SGTM and renamed *Campana*. **1951**: chartered to Chargeurs Réunis for Marseilles–Far East service. **1955**: sold to Sicula Oceanica and renamed *Irpinia* for Genoa–Central America service; rebuilt and lengthened. **1962**: further modernisation – single funnel installed. **1981**: withdrawn from service following inspection. **5 September 1983**: arrived at La Spezia for breaking up.

RÜGEN

January 1945: attached to Operation *Hannibal* evacuating refugees from East Prussia to Denmark. **17 March 1945**: captured by the Soviet Union. **1946**: renamed *Ivan Susanin* and placed in service on the Black Sea. **1949**: training ship for the Odessa Naval School. **1960**: discarded and broken up.

ST JULIEN

31 December 1945: arrived Southampton at end of last hospital carrier voyage and returned to Great Western Railway. **1 December 1946**: resumed Weymouth–Channel Islands service. **1948**: absorbed into the nationalised British Transport Commission fleet as a British Railways Southern Region ship. **10 April 1961**: towed to Ghent for breaking up.

Great Western Railway's *St Julien* refitting at Penarth on 17 April 1946 prior to resumption of the Weymouth–Channel Islands service. *World Ship Society*

SATURNIA

8 September 1943: made for Allies-controlled port; became a US Navy troop transport. **January 1945**: converted into a hospital ship and renamed *Frances Y. Slanger*. **November 1945**: released from hospital ship service. **February 1946**: resumed troop transportation and renamed *Saturnia*. **1 December 1946**: returned to Italia Line. **20 January 1947**: Genoa–New York service. **8 November 1955**: Trieste–New York service. **10 April 1965**: laid up at Trieste. **7 October 1965**: arrived at La Spezia for breaking up.

While in American hands, the *Saturnia* served as a troopship and then, briefly, as the hospital ship *Frances Y. Slanger*, seen here. After the war, the Italia Line restored her for transatlantic service. *Mario Cicogna*

SINAIA

August 1944: scuttled at Marseilles by retreating Germans. **9 December 1946**: refloated and broken up locally.

The *Sinaia* was scuttled at Marseilles in August 1944 by the retreating German forces. This view, dating from July 1945, shows her partially submerged with the US Navy transport *Admiral H.T. Mayo* alongside her to the left. *Jean-Yves Brouard collection*

TAIREA

1946: returned to British India Line; placed in Bombay–Durban service. **1949**: resumed Apcar service, Calcutta–Japan. **1 April 1952**: arrived at Blyth for breaking up.

TALAMBA

10 July 1943: bombed and sunk 3 miles off Avola, Sicily, during Operation *Husky*, the Allied landings on Sicily.

TALMA

October 1947: released to British India Line; placed in Calcutta–Australia service. **14 April 1949**: declared surplus to requirements; sold for demolition. **29 May 1949**: arrived under tow at Inverkeithing for breaking up.

TATUTA MARU

8 February 1943: torpedoed and sunk by USS *Tarpon* in the position 33.45N, 140.25E, 50 miles south-east of Mikura-jima, east of Honshu, while bound Yokosuka–Truk.

TEIA MARU

18 August 1944: torpedoed and sunk by USS *Rasher* 150 miles west of Cape Bolinao, Luzon, in the position 18.18N, 120.13E, while bound for Singapore in convoy HI-71.

After her mercy mission, the *Teia Maru* served as a Japanese troop transport until she was sunk on 18 August 1944. A total of 2,665 men lost their lives in the sinking. *Author's collection*

VALAYA

13 January 1944: sunk by a mine near Bangkok in the position 13.36N, 100.36E.

VULCANIA

8 September 1943: made for Allies-controlled port; became a US Navy troop transport; formally requisitioned after the war, she made six voyages for American Export Line. **14 December 1946**: returned to Italia Line. **June 1947**: single voyage Genoa–South America. **4 September 1947**: Genoa–Naples–New York service. **28 October 1955**: Trieste–New York service. **1965**: sold to Grimaldi-Siosa Line and renamed *Caribia*. **February 1966**: Southampton–Vigo–Lisbon–West Indies immigrant service and Mediterranean cruises. **23–24 September 1972**: stranded near Nice; engine room flooded. **29 September 1972**: laid up at La Spezia. **18 September 1973**: arrived at Barcelona for breaking up. **15 March 1974**: resold to Taiwanese ship-breakers and left Barcelona under tow. **20 July 1974**: sank outside harbour on arrival at Kaohsiung.

WEST POINT

22 July 1946: released from transport service, resold to United States Lines and renamed *America*. **14 November 1946**: first commercial voyage New York–Le Havre–Southampton. **25 October 1951**: transatlantic service extended, New York–Le Havre–Southampton–Bremerhaven. **November 1964**: sold to Chandris Lines and renamed *Australis*. **20 August 1965**: Piraeus–Sydney service. **16 October 1965**: Southampton–Suez-Australia–New Zealand–Panama–Southampton round-the-world service. **18 November 1977**: laid up at Piraeus. **19 May 1978**: sold to America Cruise Lines, later Venture Cruise Line; arrived New York and renamed *America*. **August 1978**: resold to Chandris Lines and renamed *Italis* for cruising; forward funnel removed during refit. **12 September 1979**: laid up at Piraeus. **May 1980**: sold to Intercommerce Corp. SA and renamed *Noga* for use as static hotel ship. **1984**: sold to Silver Moon Ferries and renamed *Alferdoss*. **1993**: sold to Chaophraya Development Corp. and renamed *American Star* for transfer to Phuket as floating hotel. **18 January 1994**: parted tow and stranded off Fuerteventura in the position 28.20N, 14.10W.

BIBLIOGRAPHY AND SOURCES

Public Archives and Official Records

Guildhall Library
Lloyds Weekly Casualty Reports (various)

International Committee of the Red Cross
Rapport du Comité International de la Croix-Rouge sur son activité pendant la seconde guerre mondiale, 1 septembre 1939–30 juin 1947 (Geneva, June 1948) – referred to in text as ICRC-1948

National Archives
ADM 1/13976 *Repatriation of 788 RN and RM personnel from Italy under special repatriation agreement*, 1943

ADM 1/15869 *Proposed exchange of civilians between Allies and Japan*, 1944

ADM 1/15885 *Exchange of diplomatic and consular staff of Germany and Argentina*, 1944

ADM 116/4682-4684 *Italian Civilians: repatriation from East Africa*, 1942–43

BT 389 series *Merchant Ship Movements cards* (various)

FCO 141/9108 *Malta – evacuation of British and Italian consuls and their staffs*, 1940

FO 369/2737 *Arrangement for evacuation of British subjects from various countries*

FO 371/31748 *Safe conducts for ships engaged in exchange voyages*

FO 371/50127-50134 *Exchanges of diplomats and officials between Allied and enemy countries*

FO 818/50 *Repatriation of British subjects*, March 1945

FO 916/356-357 *Italian and British subjects – reciprocal arrangements for repatriation*, 1942

HO 213/489 *Repatriation of Internees. German proposals for exchange of prisoners of war and civilian internees*

HO 213/1745 *Repatriation and exchange: specified German nationals in UK and British subjects in Germany; prisoners of* war in UK and Germany, 1940–41
MT 40/148 *Troopships that Survived the War*
WO 32/9374 *Conventions and International Agreements: Prisoners of War: Mixed Medical Commission*

United States National Archives & Records Administration:
R.G.26 US Coast Guard Entry 180-A1 *Merchant Vessel Information Files* (various)

Contemporary Newspaper and Magazine Articles

Daily Express
'30 Italians Change Their Minds' (18 June 1940), 'Mercy Ships to Break Black-Out' (3 October 1941), 'Berlin Delays Mercy Ships' (4 October 1941), 'Mercy Ships Go Across Today' (6 October 1941), '"Stop" Order at 1 AM' (7 October 1941) and 'Mercy Ships Empty Again' (8 October 1941)

Daily Mirror
'Berlin Message Stops Mercy Ships Leaving' (4 October 1941) and 'Mercy Ships Are Stopped by Zero Hour Phone Call' (7 October 1941)

Diário da Noite
'Intercambio de Diplomáticos Argentinos y Alemanes' (30 June 1944), 'Fase Final de la Ruptura de las Relaciones de Argentina con Alemania' (1 July 1944) and 'No Vinieron los Diplomáticos Argentines' (10 September 1944)

Diário da Notícias
'Deixam a America os Ultimos Existas' (18 July 1944) and 'Pregunta por sus Diplomáticos' (6 October 1944)

La Vanguardia
'El Canje de Prisiòneros Heridos y Enfermos, Alemanes y Británicos, en Aquas de Barcelona' (27 October 1943), 'Hoy se Efectúará el Canje Anglo-Aleman de Prisiòneros' (27 October 1943) and 'Al Amparo de la Neutralidad Española' (28 October 1943)

Lloyds List (various)

Século Illustrado
'A Troca de Prisiòneros Ingleses e Italianos em Lisboa – Portugal Oasis da Europa' (4 April 1943)

The Times
'1,500 War Prisoners Coming Home' (30 September 1941), 'Exchange of Prisoners' (4 October 1941), 'Exchange of Prisoners Again Held Up' (7 October 1941), 'No Exchange of Prisoners' (8 October 1941), 'Repatriation Frustrated' (8 October 1941) and 'Homeward Bound Prisoners' (19 October 1943)

Newsreel Films

British Pathé

Repatriation Hold-Up. Newhaven, East Sussex, 1941 (ID: 1133.08), *Repatriation of Italian Prisoners of War*. Middle East, 1942 (ID: 1326.04), *Repatriated Prisoners of War Arrive in Egypt*. Alexandria, Egypt, 1942 (ID: 1324.27), *Exchange of Prisoners*. Mersin, Turkey & Alexandria, Egypt, 1943 (ID: 1081.09), *Prisoners Exchanged*. Lisbon, 1943 (ID: 1083.05), *Blighty Ones*. 1943 (ID: 1079.04), *Happy Americans on their Way Home from Jap Prisons*. Rio de Janeiro, 1943 (ID: 1921.1 Movietone News film), *Repatriation Through Spain*. Barcelona, 1943 (ID: 1097.23), *Wounded Returning Home*, Liverpool, 1943 (ID: 1943.02), *Hospital Ship Docks at Home*. Glasgow, 1943 (ID: 1889.01 & 02), *Hospital Ship Atlantis 1940–1949*. Glasgow, 1943 (ID: 1893.06-08), *Prisoners of War and Wounded Come Home*. Liverpool, 1944 (ID: 2121.04), *Back to Blighty*. Liverpool, 1944 (ID: 1125.09), *Troops Returning Home*. Liverpool, 1944 (ID: 1887.02), *Hospital Ship Drottningholm*. Gothenburg, 1943 (ID: 1887.03), *Hospital Ship Docks at Home*. Liverpool, 1944 (ID: 1887.08 &09) and *Hospital Ship Atlantis*. Liverpool 1944 (ID: 1887.06)

Critical Past Historic Stock Footage

Japanese civilians embark aboard Red Cross ship Gripsholm at New York Harbor as Part of Exchange and Repatriation Agreements, 1943 (film in six parts) and *Americans Home from Nazi Prisons – the Gripsholm Arrives in New York Harbor*, March 15, 1944 (video 65675021166)

HBO Archives

No title: *Drottningholm* at New York, 1 June 1942 (March of Time film footage, reference 4931006_014 & 4932934383_015)

War Office Film Unit
Wounded Italian Prisoners Arriving at Alexandria Docks for Repatriation, 15 April 1943 (Imperial War Museum catalogue no. AYY 427/2) and *Repatriated British Prisoners Arrive in Port Said*, 1943 (Imperial War Museum catalogue no. ADM 534)

YouTube video
Gripsholm lands at New York with former internees of Santo Tomas Internment Camp, Manila, 1943

Other Published Sources and Websites

Arnold Hague Convoy Web, Ship Movements (http://www.convoyweb.org.uk)

Cernuschi, Enrico, Brescia, Maurizio & Bagnasco, Erminio, *Navi Protette*, appendix from *Le Navi Ospedale Italiane, 1935–1945* (Societa Italiana di Storia Militare, Parma, 2010)

Combined Fleet, *Kokansen* (www.combinedfleet.com/kaigun.htm)

Corbett, P. Scott, *Quiet Passages* (Kent State University Press, Ohio, USA, 1987)

Isherwood, John H., *Steamers of the Past* articles in *Sea Breezes* (various from January 1951 to December 1987)

Kludas, Arnold, *Great Passenger Ships of the World*, vols 1–4 (Patrick Stephens, 1975–77

Kohler, Peter C., *The Lido Fleet – Italian Line Passenger Ships & Services* (Seadragon Press, 1998)

Komamiya, Shinshichiro, *Senji Yuso Sendan Shi* [Wartime Transportation Convoys History] translated by William G. Somerville, England (Shuppan Kyodosha, Tokyo, 1987)

Miller, David, *Mercy Ships* (Continuum Books, 2008)

Salships, *Drottningholm & Gripsholm Exchange & Repatriation Voyages During WWII* including *From Prisoners of War to War Brides* (www.salship.se/)

Tucker, Robert W., *The Law of War & Neutrality at Sea* (1955, republished by The Lawbook Exchange, Clark, New Jersey, 2006)

Valenti, Paolo, *I Quattro Conti* (Luglio Editore, Trieste, 2011)

———, *La Grandi Unità* (Associazione Marinara 'Aldebaran', Trieste, 2005)

———, *Le Quattro Sorelle* (Luglio Edizioni, Trieste, 2007)

Valenti, Paolo & Zorini, Decio, *Saturnia & Vulcania* (Societa Italiana di Storia Militare, Parma N.35 Vol. IV August 1996, pp. 31–40)

Ward, Rowena, *The Asia-Pacific War and the Failed Second Anglo-Japanese Civilian Exchange* (The Asia–Pacific Journal, Vol. 13, Issue 11, March 2015)

Williams, David L., *Dictionary of Passenger Ship Disasters* (Ian Allan, 2010)

———, *In Titanic's Shadow* (The History Press, 2013)

Winser, John de S., *Short Sea, Long War* (World Ship Society, 1997)